HANDBOOK
FOR
Youth Discipleship

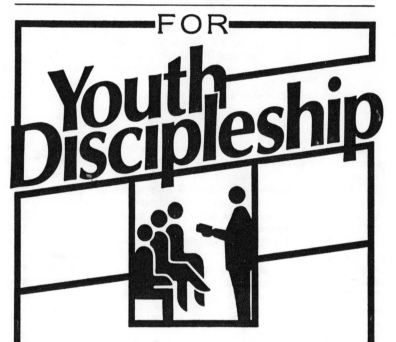

R. Clyde Hall, Jr.
Compiler/Contributor

BROADMAN PRESS
Nashville, Tennessee

ISBN: 0-8054-6003-9
Dewey Decimal Classification: 268.433
Subject Headings: DISCIPLESHIP // YOUTH
Library of Congress Catalog Card Number: 87-30903

Printed in the United States of America

LIBRARY OF CONGRESS
Library of Congress Cataloging-in-Publication Data

Handbook for youth discipleship / R. Clyde Hall, Jr., compiler, contributor.
    p.   cm.
Bibliography: p.
ISBN 0-8054-6003-9 (soft)
    1. Church work with youth—Handbooks, manuals, etc.   2. Christian education
of young people—Handbooks, manuals, etc.   3. Youth—Religious
life—Handbooks, manuals, etc.   I. Hall, R. Clyde.
    BV4447.H294 1988
259'.2—dc19   87-30903
                                                                          CIP

Foreword

I am grateful to Clyde Hall who, as a leader in youth discipleship, saw the need to compile a youth discipleship handbook. This is a comprehensive guide to developing a New Testament discipleship program for youth in the local church.

Jesus called His followers to be disciples. He intends for all who follow him to be disciples. The Greek word translated "disciple" is *manthano* which means to be a learner, to increase knowledge, to be a pupil who follows the teachings of someone else. To be a disciple of Jesus, one must follow His precepts, instructions, and example. An ancient definition said that discipleship was thought accompanied by endeavor. The one imperative in Matthew 28:19-20 is *matheteusate* (make disciples), which surely includes the entire process of winning persons to Christ and helping them to grow as Christians. The three participles in the Great Commission, "going" and "baptizing" in verse 19 and "teaching" in verse 20, spell out in greater detail the task of making disciples. The command is very clear. We are to make disciples and help them to learn and grow in the Lord Jesus. Evangelism that stops short of discipleship training has failed.

The mortality rate for new converts is high. Twenty-nine percent of Southern Baptist membership is presently nonresident and 20.5 percent is inactive. The church must accept responsibility for this failure. Discipleship training corrects this problem. The biblical mandate is clear. We begin the Christian life as babes (1 Cor. 3:1). But we must grow beyond that point or be guilty of immaturities that damage the fellowship and influence of the church (1 Cor. 2:10-13;

3:3-4; Heb. 5:12-13). Poorly grounded church members, devoid of confident faith, fall victim to doctrinal heresies (Eph. 4:14). Healthy infants grow through proper nourishment, and a recurring appetite ensures steady advance in biblical knowledge and kingdom righteousness (1 Pet. 2:2-3; Matt. 5:3,6). Christians are like athletes in training for a contest; they are like new recruits undergoing discipline and training so that they will be effective soldiers (2 Tim. 2:3-5). They are disciples who are in process of becoming like their Master (Luke 6:40). This book will provide the best thinking—thoughts of some of the finest youth leaders in America—to help you develop a discipleship process among the youth in your church.

Roy Edgemon, Director
Church Training Department
The Sunday School Board of the
Southern Baptist Convention

Introduction

Handbook for Youth Discipleship is a compilation of essays on subjects relevant to youth and youth's discipleship development. For the purpose of this book, Christian discipleship, and, therefore, youth discipleship, is defined as the "Christian's lifelong commitment to the person, teaching, and spirit of Jesus Christ. Life under Jesus' Lordship involves progressive learning, growth in Christlikeness, application of biblical truth to every area of life, responsibility for sharing the Christian faith, and responsible church membership."[1]

The book is divided into two parts, Foundations and Approaches. Part I has three sections: Theological Foundations, Philosophical Foundations, and Developmental Foundations. Part II, Approaches, includes a discussion of youth discipleship methods and youth discipleship strategies. The writers were given the freedom to develop their essays out of their own experience and expertise. A section at the back of the book gives brief biographical data on the contributors.

The purpose of this book, therefore, is to provide resources to help youth ministers, youth directors, and all youth leaders in a church with the task of equipping youth for discipleship. Nineteen persons have collaborated and contributed to the book. They hope that out of these writings new insights, new challenges, as well as a review of the familiar, will be the ground out of which much fruitful work in the area of discipling youth can grow.

I am especially greatful to my wife, Mildred, for her continued support and patience not only in the preparation of this book but also in other assignments that take me to other parts of the nation and world on behalf of training church leaders in youth discipleship methods and strategies.

I feel especially fortunate to have been professionally related for more than twenty years to an organization which has as its chief function the equipping of disciples and to be directly related to youth discipleship development for more than ten years. Out of this environment I have found fulfillment in living out my calling.

R. CLYDE HALL, JR.

Note

1. From *Church Base Design 1986 Update,* II: 51. © Copyright 1986 The Sunday School Board of the Southern Baptist Convention. All rights reserved.

Contents

Part II: Approaches

1
A Theology
of Youth Discipleship
John Hendrix

"Come and see" is an invitation to personal relationships, experiential learning, meaningful activity, and self-discovery. Jesus' call, "Follow me," led the disciples into experiences where they learned for themselves in the company of others. The compelling invitation to "come" was the magnetic attraction to be with Him and share His ministry. The simple words "to be with him" (Mark 3:14) meant that Jesus desired true companionship and fellowship. Discipleship, thus, involved a radical decision to be with Jesus.

The disciples witnessed the work of Jesus and began to do what they saw Him do. Jesus' disciples were expected to share His positive concern for people. This emphasis was expressed in Jesus' words to Simon and Andrew: "Come ye after me, and I will make you to become fishers of men" (Mark 1:17, KJV). To be with Him was to participate in a work similar to that of Jesus. This concern was evidenced in the presence of Jesus' disciples when He feasted with sinners (Mark 2:15 *ff.*), when He fed the hungry (Mark 6:34 *ff.*), and when He received a Gentile woman (Mark 7:26 *ff.*). In being with Him, they were also called to be with one another. Discipleship training takes place in the basic relationships of a small group. A group must be small enough for significant relationships between people to develop.

Jesus probably had many reasons for chosing twelve men to be with Him in a special way. We can be acquainted with many people. But the experience of caring, support, and deeper sharing can only be experienced with a few people. The first ventures into discipleship are "tried out" in the safe environments of a small group where youth are loved and where they are willing to risk themselves. Only after "testing" themselves in this way are they willing to move out into the broader dimensions of their daily living. Even then, they have the assurance that if they fail they have a group where they can find acceptance and healing for their wounds.

Training the Powers of Observation

Youth discipleship begins with training the powers of observation. That comes naturally for youth. The Youth Department first saw Julie when she was promoted from the sixth grade in October. She was quiet and hesitant, uncertain of this new world of youth ministry in the church. The youth minister didn't know her name for several months. Julie's Sunday School teacher finally pointed out the new seventh grader to the youth minister and simply said, "That's Julie." She stood quietly in the halls before Sunday School, taking it all in, as if some inner voice was tugging at her to "come and see." This gives us some of the first hints about youth discipleship development. Youth spend much time just "looking."

Julie entered the youth ministry with whatever answers and whatever unresolved questions had occurred in her past, such as relations to persons, especially her mother and father. She also came with "live" feelings about herself as an "I," her relationship to those of the same and opposite sex, and her relationship to authority. She also came with that strange mixture of wanting acceptance and affirmation and, at the same time, fearing that she would be noticed. This strange ambivalence at wanting to be seen and yet not being too visible is characteristic of young teens.

Julie entered young adolescence with bits and pieces of experiences, memories, and thoughts. It was time for her to achieve some level of commitment. Commitment is claiming ownership of one's faith in relation to the faith that has been surrounding the person during the formative years. Julie was beginning to say, "I see it, and it is mine."

Although Julie was seeing much, those things "not seen" formed the underpinnings of her faith. Julie's task, like others her age, was to form some basic level of commitment, to bring together, bind, pledge, and engage herself in the active youth ministry of the church. For young people to commit, they must be given enough freedom from the ties that kept them attached in the past so that they can be brought into the keeping of the sovereignty of God. They are now entering a new stage of life.

This act of giving Julie to another phase of the church's life should be observed by the church in a significant way because Julie and her friends are moving through a new passage that calls for both pledge and promise. They are tuning into a different network of relationships. If they can initially be faithful "in that which is least," they might eventually be faithful in much (Luke 16:10, KJV). In Julie there is the promise of things hoped for. This initial commitment and promise provides the substance or the assurance of things hoped for but not seen.

The first disciples of Jesus followed the dictates of feelings that had been awakened in them by what they saw. When young adolescents hear that compelling invitation to "come and see," they are drawn to Jesus through observation. The first lesson in discipleship, then, are lessons of hearing and seeing. Adolescents are like children born into a new world where the sights and sounds of the realm of the Spirit become real. We should not be surprised when their eyes are filled with wonder; for many of them, the longer they live the more they will acknowledge the truth of Jesus' words, "Blessed are the eyes which see the things that ye see" (Luke 10:23, KJV).

When youth move through the adolescent years, something happens to them. They expand their ability to see into things, to examine and probe and study and turn things over in their minds. In developmental terms, they are learning to think abstractly and solve the problems that face them. Things are happening in the balance between industry (I can see a way to do things and do them) and inferiority (nothing becomes clear, and I can't do anything well).

The skills that must be sharpened are the skills of observation. Youth who are entering the youth ministry of the church need a lot of experiences in observing. They need to see people who can be trusted. They need to have their thoughts and ideas accepted no matter how ludicrous they appear. They need activity where they can simply observe what is going on without having to verbalize a lot of what they are seeing.

The best things we can do to help youth see everything is to help them become fully present to every situation. Observation means bringing our whole selves in an authentic way to what is happening. Youth have a natural openness to the things happening around them. They observe, listen, and let in the signals which communicate what they are experiencing. We can help them by stripping away the barriers which keep them from seeing, hearing, and understanding. Humanly speaking, they bring their full senses into operation. Beyond this, they open themselves to the illuminating power of the Holy Spirit who can help them with those signals too subtle for human detection.

Seeing and Experiencing

Youth embody the importance of seeing discipleship in action. Often they seem to be detached and uninvolved, as if they are just watching. Come and see is an invitation to take advantage of this powerful way that Jesus taught the disciples. Disciples of Christ must come to know Him experientially before they can explain their faith intellectually. The sequence of this process is important to remember. Experience comes before intellectual assent.

Jesus refused to let the disciples intellectualize the lessons He taught them. He constantly involved them in learning experiences. The first lessons of the kingdom are lessons of seeing. The disciples saw Jesus heal the sick, touch the untouchable, comfort the broken-hearted, befriend the lonely, and forgive the guilty. When He taught lessons about prayer, He simply prayed. When He taught about servanthood, He washed the disciples' feet. He constantly urged His followers to see things which normally went unnoticed.

Sometimes He did this by calling the disciples' attention to specific things in their environment: "Do you see these great buildings?"

(Mark 13:2). "Behold, a sower went forth to sow" (Matt. 13:3, KJV). "Lift up your eyes, and see how the fields are already white for harvest" (John 4:35). By example He showed them how to see persons in the midst of multitudes, focusing on a lame man at the pool of Beth-zatha, singling out a grief-stricken woman in a funeral procession on a busy road, and spotting Zacchaeus crouching in a tree above crowds of parade watchers.

The secrets of the kingdom do not come easily. Youth do not always understand what they are seeing, but the imprint is made. The memory of those visual images remain. When all of these experiences come together, the secrets of kingdom life begin to open up. Jesus challenged the disciples to see with understanding. He was as concerned about the disciples' spiritual insight as He was about their physical eyesight. "To you it has been given to know the secrets of the kingdom of heaven, but to them it has not been given. . . . because seeing they do not see, and hearing they do not hear, nor do they understand" (Matt. 13:11,13). This perception of the spiritual reality of things brought God's presence and favor. "Blessed are your eyes, for they see" (Matt. 13:16).

The early church placed a great premium upon seeing and experiencing. John's first letter begins with the statement that John was an eyewitness and experienced firsthand the life of Jesus (1 John 1:1-3). Luke's Gospel account was written after listening to those who "from the beginning were eyewitnesses and ministers of the word" (Luke 1:2).

Youth discipleship will deal with concrete rather than abstract issues. The teachings of Jesus abound in word pictures drawn from common life—things that could be seen and touched. The Sermon on the Mount and the parables were expressed in word pictures drawn from common life. These illustrations were verbal video messages: seed and salt, vine and fig, bird and moth, dog and swine, sheep and wolf. Jesus used familiar sights and sounds as a foundation for a larger and more fascinating spiritual truth. Clear, simple truths must be understood if discipleship is to result. Jesus used the common everyday events of people to make truth relevant, calling people to the present situation.

The parables of Jesus keep calling us to see more than had previously been observed. To fully observe we open ourselves to seeing that which may be different and potentially transforming. The parable in its spoken form, art form, and action form provides the most dynamic kind of learning methodology for youth. Storytelling, "action parables," simulations, structured experiences, and learning games provide youth with meaningful activity and self-discovery, both of which are necessary in an invitation to "come and see."

In these types of activity, youth begin to use an emerging developmental ability of reflecting on what they are seeing. Reflection brings about an awareness of the meaning of learning for me. It is in a form and shape that is mine; therefore, I can act on it.

The debriefing process is crucial to helping youth understand what they are seeing. Reflection requires a deliberate and disciplined effort to stop the action long enough to ask, What is happening? When that process is followed, all youth "activity" provides potential for discipleship training. In human relations training, this process is called "I-A-G-ing" or identifying, analyzing, and generalizing. *Identifying* means describing the things that happen in an experience. *Analyzing* means breaking the experience down in identifiable factors that caused things to happen. *Generalizing* means to be able to make the learning applicable to other situations. These learning skills emerge developmentally during the youth years and become foundational for lifelong discipleship development.

Modeling takes advantage of the visual orientation of youth. Teachers and leaders of youth embody and demonstrate the truths they would teach. Adults and youth learn together in a relational and interpersonal environment. Discipleship is learning in a community of people who live out their faith together in an environment of acceptance, appreciation, and love.

Discipleship ministry with youth that incorporates modeling and relational activity can best be seen in the image of *apprentice*. Youth discipleship is not a theoretical discipline but a practical task of "doing the word." Come and see is an invitation to follow and imitate. The apprentice lives in a relationship where new behavior and demonstration of potential are encouraged. Disciples are encouraged to live freely and with courage. Doing assigned tasks without having to take full responsibility is part of the apprentice relationship. The apprentice has the opportunities provided by practice and by making mistakes, by making choices and gradually facing the consequences of choices.

Is there any significance in the fact that Jesus used two different words for seeing? One means simply to view or look upon while the other often means to grasp or understand the meaning of what is seen. A person may see a great surgeon perform a difficult operation and may admire the doctor's poise and skill. But those trained in the skills of observation see more. Trained medical students may understand the intricate processes involved and be helped toward the development of their own surgical skills. The disciples of Jesus not only saw His great spirit at work but also gained insight into the nature of their own ministry. Still, they did not understand! The full meaning of Jesus' words and deeds eluded them at the moment. Only through memory did His life and ministry come to be incredibly influential in later years, and so it will be with youth discipleship. We understand looking back. We drive into the future looking into the rearview mirror!

Seeing and Remembering

In recent years some of the most exciting discoveries in learning have taken place in the study of imagery. Images are those deep-seated, vivid, emotionally charged bundles of energy that have been called eidetic images. Eidetic forms are marked by or involve extraordinarily accurate and vivid recall of visual images. These images are formative learning tools which have the power of bringing things together in such a way as to move us to action. They have a way of evoking or calling back experiences that are stored permanently within us. Some experiments have shown how strong images can change the heart pulse from seventy beats per minute to one hundred and then back again.

The whole direction of a person's growth is profoundly influenced by these powerful, inner, emotion-packed images. Significant changes in persons come through some transformation or healing of these images. To set in motion a course of action, we form an image and draw on previously recorded images. The power between these images is enough to bring any action to completion. In biblical language the images were written on the heart, which is the storehouse of memory. Thus, we have been given the strong biblical imperative to remember.

Eidetic images (unique collection of significant life experiences) are powerful tools in youth discipleship. Memory is the handle to our roots and individual uniqueness. The task of youth discipleship is a task of making sense of experiences and how we see them (or understand these images). We cannot be memoryless. We unconsciously are committing our lives to memory as we go. Our brains have not only an enormous capacity to store memories but also the ability to be selective or filter experiences. What we remember from any given experience is eidetic, what we are open to or looking for in that moment. Those are the things that make lasting impressions.

The task of youth discipleship is in designing meaningful and memorable faith experiences. The shape of memory is not fully developed until mid-adulthood. But memory is made up of those experiences of childhood and adolescence. If youth have no important eidetic memories of faith, people of faith, experiences of God, worship, spiritual guidance, and direction, they enter adulthood in a spiritual vacuum. Youth who have had faith experiences will find images and memories that shaped their faith. No matter how much they try, they will not be able to shake these roots or memories. They will be a part of them wherever they go. They will reappear in many forms almost daily. Our task then is to sharpen and influence the scope of memories so that they will be powerful and significant.

"Church as usual" slips away from the memory and becomes useless in the growth of the youth disciple. Thus, the youth condemnation of a youth ministry that is boring is the most damaging of all because it defeats our ability to reawaken faith memories in young adult life. The criteria is inner significance, a memory that can be seen again in the mind's eye, not flashy or showy, but profound. The task to "come and see" is a challenging invitation to memorable experiences, events that they will call back to the mind's eye with power and significance and retell in adult life as a story that brings inner transformations to self and others.

In Alex Haley's book *Roots,* one scene is of the slave, Kunta Kinte, driving his master to a ball at the plantation house. He heard the white people's music coming from the plantation. He parked the buggy and settled down to wait for his master's return. While waiting, he heard the sounds of another kind of music coming from the slave quarters. As the slave drew closer to the sound, he recognized the music as the music of his childhood and belonging to his people. Kunta Kinte had almost forgotten. He discovered that the man playing the music was from his native home, and they talked together in his native language.

Kunta Kinte went home a changed man. He lay upon the dirt floor of his cabin, weeping in sadness that he had almost forgotten, weeping in joy that he had at last remembered. The terrifying experience of slavery had almost obliterated his memory of who he was. But the music had reawakened the memories, those visual images, forms, people, stories, and events that reminded him of who he was.

In this lesson on remembering, an image of Christy comes back to me. I worked with her three years in Youth Church Training. *Work* is the right word. It was a toilsome, fatiguing, sweating, labor of love. I remember it as one of the most demanding maieutic (midwifery) tasks of trying to give birth that I ever experienced. At the end of the three years, I could see nothing. She was still the same rebellious, resentful, obnoxious, negative influence as the first night she slouched into the back corner of the Sunday night classroom. Happily, for both of us, she went off to college, and my attention was directed elsewhere. She slipped into the "back roads" of my mind, occasionally reappearing for a moment.

Fifteen years later, she reappeared, coming back in sharp focus in soft pastel pink stationary. On the corner of the envelope was Christy's married name in a "scribble" that characterized her personality.

DEAR JOHN AND LELA,
Just saw where you were moving to Louisville to teach at the seminary. I felt this strong need to tell you how important you were to my growing up years. The things you said and did have always remained with me. I often wonder where I would be and what I would be doing without your strong presence in my life.

When all of this came back to her I do not know. But I do know the process. The images were there because for three years she came and saw. When those images and memories were critical to her growth, she remembered.

Seeing and Church Life

Come and see is the compelling invitation for youth to live out their discipleship in the weekly activity of church life. Youth become disciples through visual participation in the life and work of the church. This becomes powerfully evident through the observance (the "seeing") of three historical symbols: baptism, the Lord's Supper, and the Lord's Day.

What does a church mean when believers say, "We are going to observe baptism and the Lord's Supper"? What are the meanings of these two ordinances as symbols? What is the observance of a symbol? To observe symbols is to see things that represent a concrete reality. A symbol stands for something because it stands on something. In this case, baptism, and the Lord's Supper stand on the concrete acts of Jesus in behalf of our salvation. They are "visual aids" to help us "dramatize" our relationship with Jesus.

These two symbols become powerful because they represent experiences that we know not only with our minds but with our bodies as well. In baptism we see, or observe, with our whole body the power of water and washing, of immersing and cleansing, of death and rebirth. In the Lord's Supper we observe with our whole body the touch, smell, and taste of life-giving food and drink. Both ordinances are "pictorial sermons" which help us remember Christ's life, death, resurrection, and return.

Jesus asked us to do these ordinances both for Him and with Him. When we observe these ordinances by seeing with our whole beings, we remember Jesus and He lives among us. These two ordinances provide the experiential, relational, and remembering events that provide youth the opportunities "to be with Him."

The Lord's Day has come to mean a day reserved for worshiping God and for rest. For Christians the term describes a day that belongs to God. How Christians live the Lord's Day has to do with what we see (observance) and what we remember (commemorate, memorialize).

So the Lord's Day should be full of memorable experiences, events, and people not easily forgotten. Boring and mundane experiences on the Lord's Day are faith defeating because what is seen (observed) slips quickly from the memory and commemorating the resurrection of Christ becomes impossible.

The early Christians gave evidence of the resurrection of Christ in gathering together on the first day of the week. In their gathering the presence of Christ became real, and the exhilaration and excitement of Jesus' live presence led them to shout, "It is the Lord! He is risen!" That is not easily forgotten.

In summary, youth discipleship is a deed-word combination of relationships, modeling, experiential activity, observation, reflection, and remembering. Consistent with contemporary educational understanding, genuine learning takes place when the lesson taught has direct relation to the concrete experience of the learner. This is best facilitated by processes which employ reflection upon involvement in concrete activity. These "teachable moments" are most powerfully done in community—a relational environment of love and acceptance. Contemporary education methodology has reminded us of those things. But a close examination of the New Testament will reveal those same principles in Jesus' equipping of the disciples.

2
Youth Discipleship and Faith Formation
Dan Aleshire

Jenny is nine, going on ten. She asked to talk with her mother and me the other evening, after returning from camp. She said that she had begun to understand more about what it meant to be a Christian, that she felt God speaking to her, and that she was ready to make her profession of faith. It was a marvelous night for me. We stayed up later than usual, as I told her the gospel story. It was not the first time we had talked our way around the gospel, but it was one of the more memorable times.

Jenny has been a part of a faith community since she was born. She has been Sunday Schooled, Church Trained, Ga'ed, choired, camped, and Bible schooled. She has heard the gospel a variety of ways across the years of her life. She has believed it as it was given to her. On this night, she was expressing her desire to align her life on the side of God's graceful gift in Jesus Christ. We talked about sin and repentance, acceptance and forgiveness, and a witness to God's redeeming activity through baptism. The lessons she had been learning over a lifetime were quickened by the Spirit of God, and in the summer of her ninth year, feeling and understanding merged into Jenny's profession of faith.

Jenny's story is repeated in the lives of many other Christian families as children grow in the nurture of worship and education, make their professions of faith, and are baptized into the fellowship of congregations. Persons who have grown up in the church are often nine or ten years old when they make this life-directing decision. In a few years, Jenny will enter the Youth Department at our church.

She will take the faith that has been forming through her childhood, and which she has now professed, with her. Some of the experiences of faith she will have as a youth will be influenced by the experiences she has already had, and other experiences will be in reaction to the faith she has claimed as a nine-year-old.

For most youth who grow up in the church, faith formation does not begin during youth years. Rather, it is a continuation of a work of grace that was begun earlier. This chapter examines this process of faith formation and youth by asking three questions: *What is faith? How does faith form? What kinds of movement occur in a forming faith?* Throughout this analysis, I will focus on biblical images that provide the basis for the answers. The questions are so fundamentally important, however, that Scripture provides a variety of images and explanations, and this chapter will identify only a few. I also want to identify some of the characteristic experiences which youth frequently encounter as their faith forms over time.

What Is Faith?

For by grace you have been saved through faith; and this is not your own doing, it is the gift of God—not because of works, lest any man should boast. For we are his workmanship, created in Christ Jesus for good works (Eph. 2:8-10).

These verses help us understand the context of faith, if not the character of faith itself. Faith is not something that exists apart from the grace of God. For me, faith and grace mingle so closely that, at times, it is difficult to distinguish one from the other. Whatever faith is, it exists in the embrace of the grace of God. If there were no grace, there could be no faith. While faith is something within the human spirit, it has been created by, is evoked by, and will be preserved by the grace of God.

Faith is the human response to the initiative of God in our lives, but faith is not something which human beings conjure up on their own. Faith is something which God, by grace, gives to persons. While people must assume the responsibility of stewards for the faith that is in them, faith is not a human invention.

Faith is the daily activity of remembering God and living in the awareness of the work of God.

Faith is a willingness to involve one's self in the redemptive activity of God. Faith makes a welcome place for the redemptive work of God in one's own life. (In the language of Scripture, we become the pliable resource for the "workmanship" of God.) Faith also is the commitment of individuals to join with God in God's redemptive mission to the world—reaching to people who are lost, hungry, homeless, oppressed, and devastated by the consequences of evil. (In the language of Scripture, we are "created in Christ Jesus for good works.")

Faith is a way in which individuals are given the gift of relationship with God. To be in relationship requires holding to certain truths. Relationships also require emotional commitments. Finally, relationships depend on and grow from the consistent behavior and faithful actions of the individuals involved in the relationship. The image of relationship is perhaps the most crucial one for an understanding of what faith is.

A marriage relationship illustrates well what I am saying about a relationship with God through faith. A good marriage relationship depends on husband and wife believing that certain things are true about each other: that the spouse is trustworthy, that the spouse has certain good qualities, and that the spouse will receive and respect the love that is given. If either spouse does not believe certain truths about the other, the relationship will be painfully flawed. A good marriage relationship also requires emotional commitment. It is not enough to believe that the spouse is a good person or is trustable. There must also be love. Love enhances belief in the other, but it is not the same thing as belief. Emotions connect persons in relationship differently than do ascriptions about truth. Emotions link people through the reason of the heart and by the logic of commitment. There are times in many marriages when all the beliefs about the other are called into question, but the passionate reason of the heart continues to energize the relationship. A marriage relationship also requires action—consistent, disciplined, faithful behavior. Beliefs and feelings will not maintain the relationship all by themselves. Some behavior will also be required. The behaviors include attending to one another's needs, caring for each other, and working together at the tasks for which marriage was invented.

Faith relates people to God, and a relationship with God requires: assertions about the truth in God, an emotional commitment to God, and faithful work on behalf of the purposes of God. Faith includes thinking, feeling, and doing. Faith formation involves the growth and maturing of these characteristics over time. Now, the second question comes into focus, and it deals with the processes by which formation occurs.

How Does Faith Formation Occur?

I am reminded of your sincere faith, a faith that dwelt first in your grandmother Lois and your mother Eunice and now, I am sure, dwells in you (2 Tim. 1:5).

Therefore, my beloved, as you have always obeyed, so now. . . work out your own salvation with fear and trembling; for God is at work in you, both to will and to work for his good pleasure (Phil. 2:12-13).

Faith is formed and fashioned. It is not just the same thing from the first day an individual believes until the last day that person experiences life on this earth. Faith changes. It matures. It grasps new insights and garners new commitments.

Faith is formed first of all by the abiding grace and work of God. Jesus is both the author and finisher of our faith, and the one who has begun a good work in us will continue it. Whatever else I say about the formation of faith, its foundation is best understood as fixed in God's grace.

Faith is formed in the lives of believers—both young and old— through their experiences and associations with other believers. What was true for Timothy is true for us. The "faith that dwelt first" in a grandmother and a mother now "dwells in" Timothy. It is not that faith is passed from one person to another like a possession that can be given, nor is that faith like a contagious disease that one person can catch from another. Rather, it is that the witness to God's grace and the way of faith comes through people. When incarnated in the life of the faithful believer, faith is made manifest, tangible, and touchable. It can be seen and felt, and the way of faith can be learned.

The faith of youth is formed, at least in part, as they have the opportunity to share experiences with others—young and old—who are people of faith. Just as the gospel is made flesh in Jesus of Nazareth, so the work of grace is made manifest in the faithful lives of those whom God is redeeming. Youth pay close attention to the adults who are in the church. When youth witness the authentic presence of faith, it registers with them; and they will sometimes seek to pattern their lives after the people whose faith impressed them. Faith calls youth to pattern their lives after the Christ, and persons who embody Christlike ways help youth better understand how to pattern their lives after Christ.

Another way in which faith is formed is through the work to which the apostle Paul referred when he urged the Philippians to "work out your salvation." As youth participate in the mission of being Christian people in the world, their faith is changed and formed into new awareness and commitments. Adults in church are frequently amazed when the youth return from a mission trip or conducting a mission Vacation Bible School and tell what it meant to them. They talk about seeing their own faith in a new way or about renewed commitments to be a different kind of Christian than they have been, or about the needs they now see in the world which Christian people should address. All of these comments bear witness to the ways in which faithful work has a way of forming and fashioning faith. Adults shouldn't be so surprised. Faith is formed as youth work out their salvation.

Still another way that faith is formed is through the ongoing experience of the presence of God. Since faith is relational, it requires some time in which that relationship is the focus of attention. The faith of youth is formed as youth spend time in Bible study, in prayer and devotion, and in worship. All of these activities provide the opportunity for individuals to experience the presence of God in their lives.

People discover God's presence in other ways, of course, and youth need to be encouraged to be open to the way God speaks through events, through the created order, and through the witness of other people. In all of these, youth must learn that being present to God is not something that "just happens." They need to be open to God in a disciplined manner so there is a readiness to sense the presence of God and an ability to hear the voice of God when God speaks in subtle and quiet tones. The experience of the presence of God requires the discipline to wait before the Lord and the discipline to be open to the variety of ways in which God may choose to reveal God's own self in relationship.

As faith is formed, the way in which the individual relates to God changes. Truths are held more realistically, emotions mature into more durable and dependable dispositions, and behavior becomes more persistent. As faith forms, the thoughts, feelings, and actions of faith grow more congruent with each other. Faith reflects an increasing degree of consistency, more of the "wholeness" of which Scripture speaks. These images begin to point the way to the next question.

What Is the Direction of Faith's Formation?

Have this mind among yourselves, which is yours in Christ Jesus, who . . . emptied himself, taking on the form of a servant (Phil. 2:5-7).

The fruit of the spirit is love, joy, peace, patience, kindness, goodness, faithfulness, gentleness, self-control; against such there is no law (Gal. 5:22-23).

As youth practice discipleship seriously and intentionally, youth's faith will move in certain directions. I have already suggested that the dimensions of faith—thought, emotion, and behavior—will mature both by changing individually and growing more congruent with each other. The directions a forming Christian faith takes introduce

new emphases in an individual Christian's experience. In the midst
of the Scripture's many images, I would like to call your attention to
three.

Seeing People as Christ Saw Them

*One direction of a forming faith is that, over time, people grow more able to see
the world and its people as Christ saw them.*—The "mind of Christ," in the
language of Philippians, grows in us as grace tutors faith. As faith
forms, Christians learn more about serving others and are less inclined toward wanting others to serve them. That is a pattern of
growth in all of life, isn't it? Infants are born into the world requiring
service from parents and others who will take care of their needs. As
the children grow, they may demand that others serve them; but over
time, they learn to take responsibility for themselves. Faith is never
formed in such a way that people lose their dependence on God. But
it does form in a way that Christians find themselves both more
inclined and more capable of serving others. They grow to have the
mind of Christ. And Christ sees others as people to serve, to help, and
to love.

*Another direction in the formation of faith is that individuals grow in the
qualities, which Galatians describes as fruit of the spirit.*—Note *what* the presence of these qualities contribute to individuals' lives. They do not
enhance a person's relationship with God so much as they influence
the relationships people have with each other. The fruit of the Spirit
include qualities such as love (a fundamental way of relating to
others), patience (a way of responding to our inability to control
people or events), kindness (a style of relating to other people that
respects who they are and their rights as well as one's own needs and
rights), gentleness (a way of encountering other people that recog-
nizes that they have areas of hurt and need). These qualities emerge
in people over time as faith grows and matures. The result is that
Christian faith provides resources to treat one another with care and
integrity. As faith forms, growing Christians are motivated and en-
abled to relate to others in the ways that characterize Jesus' own
pattern of relationships.

Third, as faith forms, persons learn to long in the way that Jesus longed.
—Longings, of course, are not always good. Youth can set their hearts
on a stereo or car, on an identification with a peer group, or on
escaping their families for a questionable romantic relationship.
Longings can be destructive and misguided. Longings can also be
resources for discipleship as persons lean into the passionate longing
of God for the world and its people. Christian life is never life in
neutral. It is life in which longings and passions are maintained, even
nurtured and increased. But they are longings that are surrendered to
the purposes of the will of God.

Youth have little difficulty learning to long—to yearn for what is
not yet a part of their lives. As their faith forms in them, they will
learn to long for some of the same things for which Jesus longed. A
part of the biblical image is in the prayer that Jesus taught. The
disciple prays that God's will be accomplished on earth just like it
gets done in heaven. Another image is the one that is used in Philippians, and elsewhere, about the Christian pressing on toward the
"prize of the high calling of God in Christ Jesus" (3:14, KJV). Christian people learn to long for the dream that God has crafted.

The directions in which faith forms are many, but these three are
crucial. As faith continues to be formed in youth over time, they will
learn to see the world more in the way that Christ saw it; they will
experience the emergency of qualities in them which Scripture has
called fruit of the Spirit, and they will learn to long after the world
in the way that God does. None of these qualities is likely to grow
to maturity in adolescence. Faith is forming during the years of
youth, but it does not arrive at a final state of formation. Growth
toward Christian maturity is a lifetime phenomenon. That is why I
have chosen to talk in terms of the directions of faith formation
rather than the results of a "formed" faith.

Youth and Faith Formation

As faith is formed in the lives of youth, they often encounter some
typical questions and experiences. Helping youth with their faith
requires other Christians to be aware of these questions and sensitive

to these experiences. While the experiences and questions I want to mention are typical, they do not occur in the lives of all youth. They may be typical, but they are not required for faith to continue its journey toward maturity.

One characteristic in many youth is the sheer intensity of faith which they can exhibit. While most parents and church leaders spend much of their time worrying about those youth who seem to have no interest in the Christian life, each church frequently has youth who have a very intense form of faith. They take seriously their own sin, the destructive nature of evil in the world, their need to be involved in personal devotion as well as activities at church. At times they are very impatient with the accommodation they perceive adults have made to a less stringent and radical faith. These youth are frequently treated as if they have little or no need for nurture and guidance from adult Christians. They do, however.

They need to learn how to "ease up" on themselves at times and to experience the presence not only of God's commands but also of God's grace. They need to learn how to discipline the intensity of their religious commitments without lessening their commitments. They need to grow in the direction of patience, joy, and gentleness because intense faith in youth is frequently impatient, demanding, and hard nosed. These youth may be few in number, and they seldom attract attention in church other than the admiration of adults. They sometimes have a way of intimidating adult leadership into assuming that, even though the adults have been on the Christian journey longer, they have very little to contribute to these youths' lives. This is not true. Even intense expressions of faith are still faith experiences in formation. Adults have much to contribute. Youth with intense faith do not need for it to mellow, but they do need for it to mature and develop perspective. Some youth are blessed with a bold and adventuresome faith, and it needs steady nurturing by adult companions in faith.

Other youth encounter a very different experience of faith as they move into adolescence. They, like many others, made a profession of faith when they were nine or ten years old. They knew what they were doing, did not do it under some outside pressure, and meant what they said when they professed faith and were baptized. They come to their youth years, however, asking questions of everything. Many youth look at every idea they brought into adolescence from childhood to determine if it should be kept. It is not unlike the way many early adolescents go through their possessions. They sort through their rooms and closets and decide which things—cherished through childhood but which now seem childish—perhaps should be thrown away. Some youth go through a similar process with their own faith. They wonder if any commitment they made as children really matters now that they are older and see the world in a different way.

Adults nurture faith in formation as they help these youth with their memory. Some youth need an adult who was around years earlier and who now can remind them that they did mean what they did when they professed faith, that they were sincere, that they were sorry for their sin, and that God did enter their lives with the gift of grace. Many youth have faith that is changing from the faith they had as children, and this kind of change needs a faithful memory.

Adults should also encourage youth, in the face of their questions, to remember both what they have done in the past and what God has done as well. Their questions should not be taken as automatic indicators that they never received the gift of God's salvation. Many youth routinely take inventory of the promises and possessions they bring from childhood to the maturity of their youth years. In the process of the inventory, they frequently ask questions about the promises they have made. That they ask the questions should not be taken as evidence that they did not mean an earlier decision or that they have no faith. These youth need the encouragement to keep the promises they have made and the assurance that the God who began a good work in them will continue it.

For a third group of youth, faith seems to travel an uneven road. At camp or by the end of retreat or revival, they are as committed as anyone might hope for them to be. But a week later or a month away, they seem uninterested, distracted, even annoyed by the demands of faith in their lives. There seems to be a lack of steadiness or consistency, and both the youth and adults frequently wonder what it means. One thing it means, at least for many youth, is that faith is still forming. It is still maturing. It still needs to grow in the directions of congruence and consistency. These youth, as others, need guidance and encouragement, as well as a little patience.

Not all youth will be classified among the three typical groups I have identified. But many will. One of the reasons for all these different expressions is that faith is being formed. At every point of the way, it is altogether faith. Faith is not the end product of formation. Rather, the character of healthy faith is that it is forming—it is guided toward change as life and grace continue to work in person's lives.

3
Youth Discipleship and Spiritual Gifts
Ed Thiele

One of the most exciting aspects about youth work is helping youth discover and use their spiritual gifts. All Christian youth have one or more spiritual gifts. They need to be taught the source, nature, purpose, development, and use of their gifts.

The Bible has plenty to say about spiritual gifts, but a lot of confusion exists in our churches about them. The disturbance over glossolalia or tongues speaking is probably the main reason we have been confused and wary. The current wave of charismatic interest and activity intensifies the need for us to be better informed. Presumably, once we are better informed about the biblical message on gifts, we will be more eager to help the youth in our churches in this area.

Paul wrote to the Corinthian Christians: "Now concerning spiritual gifts, brethren, I do not want you to be uninformed" (1 Cor. 12:1). Surely God does not want any of us to be ignorant about spiritual gifts. He wants all of His children to be aware of all of His gifts, especially the spiritual ones, and to receive them happily and use them wisely.

Source of Spiritual Gifts

God is the source of spiritual gifts. James 1:17 declares: Every good endowment and every perfect gift is from above. In 1 Corinthians 12:7-11, God is the Spirit who grants varied gifts. In Ephesians 4:7-16, Jesus is the One who gives different gifts of leadership as He sees fit. While in Romans 12:6-8, divine grace is the active cause distributing gifts. God the Father, Son, and Holy Spirit act in perfect unity to equip the churches with every spiritual gift that is needed for fruitful ministry by supplying members with different spiritual abilities. We all need to worship and praise God for His wonderful provision for us.

Three major New Testament passages treat the subject of spiritual gifts. Paul was the author of each of them. In Romans 12:6-8, 1 Corinthians 12—14, and Ephesians 4:7-17 one may find most of what the Bible has to say about *charismata*, spiritual gifts. The Greek word for *grace, charis*, is the root of this word which may be rendered literally "grace-gifts." God in His matchless grace not only gives the churches what they need but also gives to individual Christians what they need to be effective members of the church.

Another stimulating aspect of a Bible study on spiritual gifts is to search out in the Book of Acts those persons who demonstrated their use of spiritual gifts. In those early days of church expansion, the Holy Spirit was in control of the lives of believers in a special way. The successful planting of churches and winning of converts in many places was clearly the work of God in the lives of gifted servants.

Since the Holy Spirit is most often thought of as the fountain from which spiritual gifts spring, a brief consideration of the Spirit's work in the life of a disciple seems appropriate at this point. He is Himself the supreme gift to the believer. Paul wrote, "Any one who does not have the Spirit of Christ does not belong to him" (Rom. 8:9). The Holy Spirit regenerates (Titus 3:5) or causes the new birth of the person who comes to Christ in faith (John 3:5-8). The Spirit likewise sanctifies or sets the Christian apart as one committed to living a holy life (1 Pet. 1:2). Furthermore, the Spirit seals the believer, guaranteeing his ultimate inheritance from God (Eph. 1:13-14). The focus of this essay, however, is that the Spirit supplies the disciple with spiritual ability to be a useful member of the body of Christ.

When Jesus calls a servant to live under His lordship, He assures that servant of the spiritual ability to do what he or she is called to do. This is best illustrated in the call of the apostles to be witnesses after the promised Holy Spirit empowered them. With the coming of the Holy Spirit upon them, they were not only able to witness but to teach, give, speak in languages they hadn't learned, and to do signs and wonders necessary in the launching of the Christian movement as well.

All that happened in the Christian community, which was first formed in Jerusalem and then multiplied in numerous locations, was attributable to the gift of the Holy Spirit Himself and the gifts He bestowed on common men and women. (Acts 2:14-21). Jesus kept His promise to His disciples that the Father would send the Spirit of truth: "He dwells with you, and will be in you" (John 14:17). They could not, as we cannot, plead inadequacy as an excuse for not fulfilling their part in His mission, for they were gifted servants of the great Lord.

The Purpose of Spiritual Gifts

Spiritual gifts are abilities given by God to do God's work in the church and in the world. They are not the same as talents. A talent is any natural ability or power; while we as Christians see it also as God given, it is not the same as a spiritual gift. J. Terry Young said, "The gifts of the Holy Spirit were privileges of calling, opportunities to exercise one's abilities under the leadership of the Holy Spirit for the benefit of the church in its ministry for Jesus Christ."[1] Only Christians may have spiritual gifts, and those which they possess may be related to their talents.

Jerry Sittser wrote: "He [the Holy Spirit] takes our bents and basic abilities, charges them with power and directs them toward the service of others."[2] I agree as long as we don't limit the Spirit to that method of operation. For example, singing is a talent which may become a spiritual gift as a Christian is able to use it under the leadership of the Spirit to inspire the church or witness to unbelievers. Speaking effectively requires natural ability which may be heightened and employed by the Spirit in the life of a believer to enable him to proclaim the gospel powerfully. This preaching of the truth then becomes a spiritual gift. Spiritual gifts relate to what we are divinely equipped to do which God can use in a spiritual ministry to others.

This does not seem comprehensive enough, though, when we are dealing with the church of the New Testament era. In regard to such gifts as healing, working of miracles, tongues, and interpretation of tongues, new powers, not directly related to inherent abilities, were manifested. Disagreement obviously prevails as to whether such new powers are still being imparted to believers today and whether the same need for them exists now as then. None of us can settle this issue for all of us.

Several types of spiritual gifts are mentioned in the New Testament. Worshiping gifts, serving gifts, witnessing gifts, and teaching gifts are the groupings used in *Master-Life* discipleship training and in the training module *Discovering Your Spiritual Gifts.* Conveniently, in these materials only sixteen charismata are included so four gifts are arranged in each of these categories. This is not without its problems, however. The gifts of faith and miracles are grouped with witnessing, for instance, and leadership is placed in the teaching category. Tongues and interpretation of tongues are omitted. Sign gifts have been clustered by some writers. Healings, miracles, tongues, and interpretation of tongues do fit well under this heading. Paul W. Powell called them "spectacular gifts"[3]

Landrum P. Leavell II classified the gifts as either teaching, communicating, or demonstrating the power of the Holy Spirit.[4] R. Wayne Jones, in his book *Using Spiritual Gifts,* placed the gifts under these labels: gifts used in the body life of the church, those used in ministry in the world, and gifts used in spiritual guidance.[5] You are free to choose from these or to invent your own. Classification does have positive value in stressing the function of gifts. The main thing is to avoid rigidity in labeling and arranging types of gifts.

Spiritual gifts are not biblically defined for us, but we must come to some understanding of terms. Dogmatism in definition should be shunned. Nevertheless, youth are apt to dismiss the whole subject if they do not understand what is being presented as it relates to their lives today.

Apostles (Eph. 4:11) were chosen by Christ and given to the church to receive and transmit the gospel as eyewitnesses of Jesus' ministry and resurrection (Acts 1:21-22). They were special messengers commissioned to preach, heal, and serve, first in a limited area (Matt. 10:5-6) and later to the ends of the earth (Acts 1:8). The church added Matthias to replace Judas (Acts 1:26) as one of the twelve. Later, Paul was made an apostle by Jesus in a postresurrection appearance (Acts 22:14-21). Some believe this completed the office of apostles, but I believe the gift of apostleship continues to be given to those who serve as missionaries and church planters. It is best seen in those who feel compelled to spread the gospel to places where it is not already being proclaimed adequately and to people of other cultures who are unevangelized.

Prophets were those given to the church to receive and declare the truth of God. The function of Old Testament prophets is well known, and prophets with new truths from God centered in the revelation of Jesus Christ were needed by the church. They still are. Preachers exercise the gift of prophecy. They speak to strengthen, encourage, and comfort believers and to build up the church (1 Cor. 14:3-5). Any member of the church may exercise this gift, not just ordained leaders (1 Cor. 14:31).

Evangelists were persons gifted in reaching the unconverted with the good news of salvation in Jesus Christ. They could gain the interest of pagans and communicate the Christian message powerfully. Both in proclamation to crowds of people and in personal address with individuals, those with the spiritual gift of evangelism were unusually effective. Their power came from the Holy Spirit. The results obtained by Peter and Paul were evidence of their possession of this gift. Ray C. Stedman offered a valuable warning, however. He wrote, "Every exercise of a spiritual gift does not produce the same result each time."[6]

The gift of pastors is one of special ability in overseeing the spiritual welfare of a group of believers over an extended period of time. It involves a leadership function and a caring role with the flock of God. The offices of bishop (1 Tim. 3:1-7), pastor, and elder (1 Pet. 5:1-3)—the three may be synonymous—were probably filled in New

Testament churches by those who conspicuously demonstrated this gift.

Teaching is another speaking gift that is vital to the church's welfare. It is the ability to instruct others in the doctrines of Christianity. Ethical principles, skills, and theological concepts will be learned usually by growing Christians from maturing believers who have this communication gift. The pastor-teacher combination is a natural one, as the listing in Ephesians 4:11 seems to indicate. I have seen many youth discover a gift for teaching during the observance of Youth Week.

The longest list of spiritual gifts is found in 1 Corinthians 12:8-10. Only two of these gifts, prophesying and teaching, are also mentioned in Ephesians 4:11. The message of wisdom and the message of knowledge were apparently both speaking gifts. The latter was aptitude in gathering and stating useful information to fellow Christians, and the former was a keenness in applying divine truth to life situations.

The gift of faith may have been supplied by the Spirit to certain believers to stimulate exalted vision and daring endeavors by the whole congregation. Any seemingly impossible achievement was seen as an attainable goal by a member with this gift.

The gift of healing (1 Cor. 12:9) may have included the ability to be a channel of God's blessings to persons with mental, emotional, spiritual, and physical illnesses so that cures were effected. Jesus restored a man's right mind, cast out evil spirits, and cured all kinds of diseases as a part of His public ministry (Mark 1:23-34; 5:1-17). The Lord continued this ministry through gifted followers after His ascension (Acts 5:12-16; 8:6-7). Many and varied are the ways Christians are used by God to heal the sick today or at least to assist in the process.

The gift of helping others is mentioned immediately after the gifts of miracle working and healing in 1 Corinthians 12:28. We are told that God appointed in the church those able to help others. Deacons certainly fulfilled that function, but so did many others. Dorcas is a good example (Acts 9:36). This gift is as greatly needed today as ever.

With lonely, bereaved, depressed, disadvantaged, unemployed, and handicapped persons all around, the church must enlist gifted helpers to constantly demonstrate love in practical deeds. Youth who have difficulty relating to the more sensational gifts should be able to see themselves readily as likely possessors of this potential for meaningful ministry.

Miraculous powers were conveyed by some as their spiritual gifts were utilized. Exactly what this means is hard to determine. Jesus walked on the water, raised the dead, and multiplied the loaves and fish to feed large crowds. Signs and wonders done by the apostles may have been similar. Paul raised a dead young man to rejoin the living (Acts 20:7-12); Peter healed a crippled beggar (Acts 3:1-10), a paralytic named Aeneas (Acts 9:32-35), and raised Dorcas to life again (Acts 9:36-42). Controversy exists concerning the prevalence of this type of miracle and this kind of gift on the contemporary scene. Nevertheless, the church should be encouraged to pray and trust God for miracles that will glorify the Lord and extend the witness of the believers.

The spiritual gift of discernment or distinguishing between spirits is always needed by spiritual leaders in the churches. Hypocrites, fakes, and evil persons who would undermine and destroy the church are found in every generation. They may appear to be benefactors and friends but are not true Christians in whom the Spirit resides. Because God loves the church, He gives the gift of discernment to one or more leaders who can deal with the deception of such persons and defend the church from error and harm.

The ability to speak in a language one had never learned and the ability to interpret a language one had never studied were spiritual phenomena experienced in first century Christianity. Ecstatic utterance which permitted spiritual interpretation is another understanding of what was practiced in the Corinthian church. A difference between the occurrence of tongues speaking in connection with evangelism in Acts and as a means of edifying the church in 1 Corinthians should be noted. In the Corinthian letter, Paul discounted the practice of speaking in tongues as a means of evangelism (1 Cor.

14:22-25) and admonished the members to use tongues speaking in the church assembly only to a limited extent when interpretation was given (1 Cor. 14:27-28). Nowhere in the New Testament is it stated that speaking in tongues was a gift given to all Christians. Rather, the reverse is true (1 Cor. 12:30).

Even though the gift of tongues and interpretation is a difficult and sensitive subject, it should be intelligently studied and calmly discussed in our churches. Youth have a right to raise their questions and engage in serious dialogue with their spiritual leaders.

The gifts mentioned in Romans 12:6-8 do not require as much definition as those in the Corinthians and Ephesians passages. They are practical in nature. Prophesying and teaching are mentioned in all three places, then, serving, encouraging, giving, leading, and showing mercy are listed. Obviously, these gifts are still needed in any church if it is to be an effective congregation. Also, these are gifts that every young person may seek and use, even if few offices in the church are open to them until later in life.

Since the spiritual gifts are to some extent different in each of the three lists already considered, I conclude with Robert E. Coleman and others that the combined list is not exhaustive.[7] The main principle is, "Now to each one the manifestation of the Spirit is given for the common good" (1 Cor. 12:7, NIV). Hence, whatever spiritual gifts will build up the church and will help it fulfill its ministry may be found among its members. For example, the ability to inspire and bless the church through singing, composing and arranging music, and playing musical instruments is a gift of the Spirit to numerous members of the churches in our time.

Paul obviously had a gift for writing that God used to build up churches. Skill in writing all kinds of Christian literature from journalistic reporting of religious events to poems, biographies, and inspirational articles and books is a valuable gift which is exhibited in the lives of many contemporary disciples.

The purpose of spiritual gifts should be kept in the forefront of our thinking: They are for the building up of the body of Christ (Eph. 4:12). This does not mean that gifted churches are to be self-centered.

Churches are built up by the Lord so that they may carry out His mission in their setting.

Gifts are not given to believers as an indication of their special favor with God or as a reward for good works. All the gifts are service gifts. Enabling members to develop in Christlikeness and competent ministry is a major reason for their presence (Eph. 4:11-13).

The way that spiritual gifts are used is also very important. Whatever gifts any member may have, he or she should use them in harmony with other members who have the same or different gifts. The strong emphasis Paul made in 1 Corinthians 13 on using whatever spiritual gifts we have with love for each other is to be frequently recalled. Without love, competition, jealousy, envy, and pride can spoil the exercise of spiritual gifts in a church.

Private use of a spiritual gift is clearly an exception to the norm as I understand the New Testament. Gifts are given to members for the sake of the whole church and are expressed in relationships. Some are best suited for use in the general assembly of believers for worship, while others may be used in one-to-one or small group relationships.

Youth ministers are not all alike, of course, and no specified list of spiritual gifts is furnished as a requirement for those who would serve in that capacity. Speaking, serving, teaching, and worshiping gifts will be useful for one who wants to assist youth in their development as disciples. The gift of encouragement which Barnabas exercised consistently is one of the most useful for a leader of youth. Providing acceptance and appreciation is a major task of one who wants to help youth discover and use their spiritual gifts.

Modeling is such an important part of a ministry to youth that spiritual fruit is as necessary as spiritual gifts in this ministry. Spiritual fruit refers to personal qualities that a Christian possesses, whereas spiritual gifts relate to one's performance. The first accents the kind of attitudes the believer displays while the latter stresses actions. Love, joy, peace, patience, kindness, goodness, faithfulness, gentleness, and self-control are the fruit of the Spirit listed in Galatians 5:22-23. The Spirit-filled life of a spiritual leader should show such fruit as well as manifesting gifts in service.

Only the Holy Spirit decides who gets what gifts and how many (1 Cor. 12:4-11). We who follow Christ are responsible, nevertheless, for what we do with the gifts we possess.

A sense of urgency should mark us regarding the use we make of our abilities. That is Peter's message in 1 Peter 4:10-11: "Each one should use whatever gift he has received to serve others, faithfully administering God's grace in its various forms. If anyone speaks, he should do it as one speaking the very words of God. If anyone serves, he should do it with the strength God provides, so that in all things God may be praised through Jesus Christ" (NIV). An accountability to our Lord as managers of spiritual gifts is a vital element in discipleship. We shall not be judged on the basis of which gifts we had but on what we did to honor and glorify God with what we received.

Learning to appreciate our own and others' spiritual gifts is a project for each disciple to undertake. Some basic steps to take and to teach others are these:

1. Get to know yourself and your abilities as well as possible.

2. Try different forms of Christian service as opportunities are presented, and evaluate your success and satisfaction in doing them.

3. Study the Bible about spiritual gifts and about those who exercised varied gifts.

4. Pray for guidance in understanding and using your gifts.

5. Ask for assistance from respected Christian friends and leaders regarding their perception of your gifts.

6. Observe the spiritual gifts of other Christians and affirm them as they employ theirs well.

Any church would be unwise to set out to duplicate all the charismata mentioned in the Bible. Some may not be appropriate or useful in a particular church. Rather, the better goal is for the members to be so attuned to the Spirit's guidance and so submissive to Christ's lordship that the church will be led to the full complement of gifts needed in that church at that time. Artificiality would likely result from efforts to find every gift in a selected body of Christians. Uniqueness among churches as well as among disciples should be respected.

Spiritual gifts already present can be developed. The preacher studies how to prepare and deliver sermons and practices using his voice properly. He is both dependent on the Holy Spirit and obligated to do his best. One with the gift of administration may learn methods of organization and how to delegate, supervise, and evaluate. Paul wrote to Timothy: "Do your best to present yourself to God as one approved, a workman who has no need to be ashamed, rightly handling the word of truth" (2 Tim. 2:15). He also instructed him: "Rekindle the gift of God which is in you" (2 Tim. 1:6). You, likewise, who are ministers to youth, will no doubt seek to arouse young disciples to apply themselves vigorously to the enhancement and exercise of their grace-gifts.

A further warning may prove helpful. The absence of a certain gift does not excuse disobedience in a disciple. Those without the gift of evangelism, for instance, are not released from their responsibility to share the gospel. Every Christian is commanded to evangelize (Matt. 28:19-20). Also, while some have the gift of giving, every member of the church has a duty to give regularly and generously (Matt. 19:8; 2 Cor. 8:7). For some, showing mercy is a service in which they excel, but all believers are under orders from the Lord to be merciful (Luke 6:36). Obedience to Bible commands must remain a high priority for all disciples of Jesus.

The calling of ministers to youth includes cooperating with the Holy Spirit in helping youth to identify, develop, dedicate, and use their spiritual gifts. Their discipleship cannot reach its potential without their awareness that they are gifted by God for His service. They must be led to experience joy in being useful in their church now and committed to continued growth in usefulness for the rest of their lives.

Notes

1. J. Terry Young, *The Spirit Within You* (Nashville: Broadman Press, 1977), p. 94.

2. Jerry Sittser, *The Adventure: Putting Energy into Your Walk with God* (Downer's Grove, Ill.: InterVarsity Press, 1985), p. 130.

3. Paul W. Powell, *Beyond Conversion* (Nashville, Broadman Press, 1977), p. 72.

4. Landrum P. Leavell, *The Doctrine of the Holy Spirit* (Nashville: Convention Press, 1983), pp. 57-58.

5. R. Wayne Jones, *Using Spiritual Gifts* (Nashville: Broadman Press, 1985), pp. 33-66.

6. Ray C. Stedman, *Body Life* (Glendale, Calif.: Regal Books, 1972), p. 42.

7. Robert E. Coleman, *The Master Plan of Discipleship* (Old Tappan, N.J.: Fleming H. Revell Company, 1987), p. 79.

4
Youth Discipleship and Evangelism
Dean Finley

The aim of this chapter is to identify the relationship of evangelism and discipleship and the implications of that relationship for ministering to youth. Given different definitions of evangelism and discipleship this becomes a difficult task. Therefore, evangelism is defined as "the verbal declaration of the gospel by a Christian along with any action aimed at reconciling a non-Christian to God." How does evangelism differ from discipleship? Which do we do first, evangelism or discipleship? The Scripture gives us two primary examples to answer these and other questions related to the relationship of discipleship and evangelism.

Jesus' Example

Did Jesus first evangelize persons and then disciple them, or did He disciple them and through the process of discipleship evangelize them? When was Jesus doing evangelism, and when was He doing discipleship? Evangelism culminates with non-Christians' confessing their sin and submitting their lives to the lordship of Christ. This is a specific act on the part of the non-Christian that can be identified at a point in time. Is it possible to identify the point in time the disciples responded to Jesus in repentance and submitted their lives to His lordship and secured their salvation? Was it at the time of their calling? Was it after His resurrection? Was it at the Day of Pentecost?

It might be helpful to pick out a specific person Jesus dealt with, for example, Simon Peter. If a person is converted at a point in time, then at what point did Peter become a Christian? Was it when Andrew brought him to Jesus (John 1:40-42)? Did he become a Christian when he dropped his net (Matt. 4:18-20)? Did he secure his salvation when he professed Jesus as the Christ (Mark 8:28-30)? How do we explain Jesus rebuking Peter three verses later (Mark 8:33) and calling him Satan? If Peter were saved before the crucifixtion, how can we explain his denial of Jesus (John 18:25-27)? Also, how can we explain Peter's salvation before Jesus' atoning death on the cross? If Peter were saved before the "It is finished" of the New Covenant, was his salvation akin to the Old Covenant of Abraham? Maybe Peter became a Christian on the Day of Pentecost when he was filled with the Holy Spirit (Acts 2:14-38)? However, if Peter had died before Pentecost would he have spent eternity separated from God? While Jesus was with Peter, was He discipling or evangelizing him?

Which did Jesus do first with His followers, discipleship or evangelism? The answer is yes! Which comes first in relating to non-Christian youth, evangelism, or discipleship? The answer is again yes! To separate evangelism from discipleship is impossible. They are so closely interwoven that the two cannot be separated. However, they are not just two different words for the same action. Some significant differences are revealed in a study of the New Testament. If youth leaders are going to have an effective evangelism and discipleship program, they should be aware of these differences.

The New Testament Church's Example

William Barclay said that there are basically four types of preaching in the New Testament: *didache*, "teaching"; *paraklesis*, "exhorting"; *homilia* or application to "life-style"; and *kerygma*, "the announcing of the good news."[1] *Kerygma* has been identified as the act of proclaiming the good news for the purpose of evangelization. *Didache* is identified with the process of teaching the related doctrines of this good news. What did the New Testament church do first in its task of disciple making? The examination of the two words *kerygma* and *didache* gives us some definite insights into this question.

In many cases the *New American Standard Bible* (NASB) translates the Greek word *kerygma* as preaching (Matt. 3:1; 12:41; Mark 1:4,7,14,39;

Luke 3:3; 4:44; 8:1; 11:32); or it will translate the word as proclaim (Matt. 10:27; Mark 1:45; 5:20; 7:36; Luke 4:19; 9:2). A second significant Greek word *euaggelion,* from which we get our word *evangelism,* is also translated by the NASB as preaching (Acts 5:42; 8:4,12,25,40; 10:36; 11:20; 15:35; 17:18). The key question is, What did the disciples preach? In other words, What was the message that they announced and proclaimed as they did evangelism? If this were an important message for the New Testament church, it should be a central message found throughout the youth ministry of a church.

A classic scholarly work related to the preaching of the New Testament church is entitled *The Apostolic Preaching* by C. H. Dodd. In this book, Dodd identified a common content in the preaching of Peter, Paul, and others. The earliest example of New Testament evangelism is Peter's announcement at pentecost in the second chapter of Acts. Later in Acts 3, Peter again preached a similar sermon. A study of these sermons reveals a developing theological concept. T. C. Smith isolated two common elements, including the place of prophecy and the call to repentance.[2] Frank Stagg identified Peter's major concern as dealing with the scandal of the cross.[3] Stagg recognized that this preaching falls into at least five major identifiable parts: the fulfillment of prophecy, the innocence of Jesus, Jesus' death as part of a divine plan, the resurrection, and the fact that all of this was witnessed by many.[4]

A close examination of these sermons and others reveals a theological concept expressed in a well-defined set of points. This is not a new idea, for even the most novice of scholars can distinguish some of the common elements in the text. However, consider the following kerygmatic summaries by biblical scholars:

C. H. Dodd[5]
1. Jesus' fulfillment of prophecy
2. Jesus' life, death, and resurrection
3. Jesus is exalted
4. The Holy spirit is with the church
5. Jesus will return

6. Call to repentance

C. S. C. Williams[6]
1. Jesus' fulfillment of prophecy
2. Jesus' passion and resurrection
3. Jesus is with God
4. Apostolic witness of these facts
5. Advent and judgment
6. The need for repentance and baptism

G. Campbell Morgan[7]
1. Jesus is named.
2. Jesus was perfect.
3. He was killed.
4. He was raised from the dead.
5. He fulfilled all prophecy.
6. He was exalted.
7. He has given His followers the Holy Spirit.

William Barclay[8]
1. Jesus' fulfillment of prophecy
2. Jesus' resurrection is proof of God's plan.
3. The crime of those who killed him
4. The cross was no accident.

R. R. Williams[9]
1. Fulfillment of Old Testament prophecy
2. Jesus is exalted.
3. Holy Spirit is a sign of power.
4. Jesus will return quickly.
5. All must repent and believe.

Frank Stagg[10]
1. Jesus was true to the prophets.
2. Jesus is risen.
3. The personal witness of the speaker

Robert Bartels[11]

1. Prophecy fulfilled in Jesus
2. The ministry of Jesus
3. His death and resurrection
4. Christ as Judge and Savior
5. The call to repentance
6. The apostles were witnesses.

In general, we can conclude that the early apostolic preaching is summarized in 1 Corinthians 15:3-8:

> I delivered to you as of first importance what I also received, that Christ died for our sins according to the Scriptures, and that He was buried, and that He was raised on the third day according to the Scriptures, and that He appeared to Cephas, then to the twelve. After that He appeared to more than five hundred brethren at one time, most of whom remain until now, but some have fallen asleep; then He appeared to James, then to all the apostles; and last of all, as it were to one untimely born, He appeared to me also (NASB).

This brief passage is the *kerygma* of the New Testament and must be the message of an effective youth ministry.

The evangelistic announcement of the New Testament church can be summarized in eight basic statements. Keep in mind that Acts is the historical account of Jesus' disciples fulfilling the Great Commission. Jesus made disciples so they could announce to the world the good news, the *kerygma*, of God's redemptive goodness.

The first kerygmatic element we can identify is the inevitable signs, wonders, and circumstances that provided an opportunity for the proclamation of the gospel (Acts 2:12; 3:9; 4:7; 8:31; 10:33; 17:19; 24:10; 26:1). Often this proclamation is in direct response to an invitation (Acts 13:15; 14:1; 17:2; 17:10,17; 18:4,19). These circumstances supply the background for New Testament evangelism. The question for youth leadership is, What is God doing in our youth ministry that provides a platform for declaring the gospel?

Second, New Testament evangelism included the fact that Jesus was the fulfillment of Old testament prophecy. The following passages attest to that fact: Acts 2:17; 3:18,22; 4:11; 7:48; 10:43; 15:15; 24:14; 26:22; 26:27; and 28:23. This data is so important, especially in the preaching to the Jewish people, because it formed the basis of an apologetic. Good evangelism is always related to the needs, understandings, and background of the listeners. Youth leaders who plan to reach and teach youth must translate the gospel into the youth culture. This process of evangelism must be closely related to the teaching ministry of the church and must avoid a quasi-parachurch theology. New Testament Christians began where their listeners were and continued to maintain a relationship to the organized established church in the Temple and synagogues. The New Testament Christians were "making disciples" by teaching non-Christians everything Jesus had taught them.

Third, New Testament evangelism proclaimed the last week of Jesus' life known as the Passion. Acts 2:23; 3:15; 3:18; 4:10; 5:30; 7:52; 10:39; and 26:23 all relate to the sacrificial, Suffering Servant motif. Jesus gave His life as a ransom for all. He was the ultimate sacrificial lamb. "In Him we have redemption through His blood, the forgiveness of our trespasses, according to the riches of His grace" (Eph. 1:7, NASB). This is why the Passion is paramount to the New Testament evangelism. Without this teaching, there would be no evangelism, that is, redemptive theology or hope. Youth must be taught the significance of God's love for them through the act of Jesus' death. In recent years, we have heard much about youth's struggle with self-image. The Passion of Jesus tells youth that they are so valuable to God that He allowed His only Son to die for them.

Fourth, New Testament evangelism revolves around Jesus' resurrection. Acts 1:21-22; 2:23-24; 2:31-32; 3:14-15; 3:26; 4:2,10; 5:30; 7:56; 10:39-41; 13:29-31; 24:15; and 26:22-23 are all passages that attest to the fact of the resurrection. The resurrection is the most important fact of the New Testament evangelism. Brenard Ramm said, "In Acts one, Luke tells us that Jesus showed himself alive by many infallible proofs, *(en pollois tekmeriois)*, an expression indicating the strongest type of legal evidence."[12] Clearly the apostle Paul taught the resurrection and its importance as he discipled others.

But if there is no resurrection of the dead, not even Christ has been raised; and if Christ has not been raised, then our preaching is vain, your faith also is vain. Moreover we are even found to be false witnesses of God, because we witnessed against God that He raised Christ, whom He did not raise, if in fact the dead are not raised. For if the dead are not raised, not even Christ has been raised; and if Christ has not been raised, your faith is worthless; you are still in your sins, (1 Cor. 15:13-17, NASB).

Youth must be taught that Christianity is not just another religion or philosophical idea among many. Christians are people who serve a risen Savior who is in the world today giving meaning, hope, and purpose to all of life.

The fifth element of New Testament evangelism is found in Acts 1:9; 2:33; 3:21; 5:31; and 10:40. These passages tell us that Jesus has been exalted and now reigns with God. Christianity teaches that the Lord Jesus Christ is the only Mediator between us and our Creator. Jesus could have come to earth, died, and been resurrected, yet if He did not become our exalted Intercessor, we would still be left in estranged relationship to God. The fact that Jesus is exalted is the basis for youth to be involved in worship. Youth who possess this knowledge will find that the fellowship of the church becomes a celebration, not boring ritualism.

A sixth element of New Testament evangelism is the proclamation of Jesus' eminent return for His followers. Acts 1:11; 3:21; 10:42; 24:15; 26:23 are all passages that record the New Testament Christians' concern with Jesus' second coming. Jesus Himself taught this, and He expected His followers to teach all that He had taught. Today's youth need to hear the words of Jesus about His second coming. They need to be aware that Jesus did intend for His followers to watch for "the signs of His coming."

These six elements of New Testament evangelism were proclaimed by the apostles because they witnessed them. The apostles wanted their listeners to know this was something they had seen and heard. Acts 3:15; 5:32; 10:39; and 13:31 tell us that the apostles declared eyewitness accounts.

What was from the beginning, what we have heard, what we have seen with our eyes, what we beheld and our hands handled, concerning the Word of Life—and the life was manifested, and we have seen and bear witness and proclaim to you the eternal life, which was with the Father and was manifested to us—what we have seen and heard we proclaim to you also, that you also may have fellowship with us; and indeed our fellowship is with the Father, and with His Son Jesus Christ. And these things we write, so that our joy may be made complete. And this is the message we have heard from Him and announce to you, that God is light, and in Him there is no darkness at all" (1 John 1:1-5, NASB)

The disciples had seen with their own eyes, had heard with their own ears, and had been transformed from a scattered bunch of individuals to a powerful evangelistic tool. Their eyewitness accounts provided for them and their listeners an absolute factual frame of reference. This eyewitness testimony is the seventh element of New Testament evangelism. A central ingredient in youth evangelism is young people who have had an "eyewitness" personal encounter with God and are taught how to share that experience.

The final New Testament evangelism element was the call to repentance, belief, and many times baptism. Acts 2:38; 3:19; 7:51; 10:43; and 13:38 tell us that those who heard the message were called upon to respond to the message. This was the purpose of the New Testament evangelistic declaration. "It is the power of God for salvation" (Rom. 1:16, NASB).

These eight elements make up the basis for all of evangelism. We can declare with assurance the good news that Jesus has had victory over death. The foundational teaching for making disciples is the kerygmatic content. James Stewart said,

The surest way to keep your ministry living and vigorous and immune from the blight of spiritual lassitude and drudgery is to draw continually upon the unsearchable riches which in Christian doctrine are lying to your hand; and to remember that you—no less than the New Testament preachers are commissioned for the purpose of kerygma, the proclamation or news, the heralding of the wonderful works of God.[13]

The front door to the making of disciples is evangelism.

However, the disciples did more than just declare the kerygmatic content. New Christians needed instruction on how to live. The disciples had heard Jesus' "new commandments" and were instructed to "teach whatsoever" they had been commanded. The word *didache* is the key word for those concerned with discipleship. Jesus was a teacher. If He were to fill out a credit card application, when asked for vocation He would write "Rabbi," meaning teacher. The New Testament is filled with Jesus' teachings, and these teachings were the focal point of His time with His disciples. Basically, the word *didache*, or Greek root word *didasko* meaning "teaching," is found fourteen times within the Book of Acts (4:2; 5:25,28 twice; 5:42; 13:12; 15:35; 17:19; 18:11,25; 20:20; 21:21; and 28:31).

In general we can make three conclusions about the use of the word *didache* in the New Testament. One, the use of the word is not restricted to a single teaching or doctrine. Two, *didache* is a word used by Luke to refer to not only the teachings of Jesus but also to Jesus' life. Three, the *didache* or teachings of the early church often included the *kerygma* but went beyond its limited content.

The disciples were concerned that the new Christians not only respond in repentance and faith but also that they live by the teachings of Jesus. Following the declaration and response of three thousand to the *kerygma*, the disciples helped the new converts to continue "devoting themselves to the apostles' teaching and to fellowship, to the breaking of bread and to prayer" (Acts 2:42, NASB). As a result of this, the New Testament church was "praising God, and having favor with all the people. And the Lord was adding to their number day by day those who were being saved" (Acts 2:47, NASB). The disciples did evangelism by declaring the *kerygma*, then they made disciples of these new converts. In the process of making disciples, the new converts evangelized others.

In summary, the *kerygma* is the good news that teenage Christians have to declare to non-Christian youth. The *kerygma* is identified as the story of Jesus' prophetic birth, life, teachings, death, resurrection, glorification, and second coming. This is the unique story of Christianity. This is the story told by the evangelist. This is the heart and soul of witnessing and all attempts to reconcile a lost world to Jesus. The *didache* gives us instructions on how to live, and much of it is not unique to New Testament Christianity. However, no other religion or philosophy includes the incarnation and resurrection of the almighty God. The *kerygma* is the identifying face of Christianity. It is the head of Christian theology, but it is filled out by the *didache* or teachings of Jesus. We might ask, What good is a head without a body, or what good is a body without a head? Both body and head are necessary to have a living, breathing organism. Christian theology is both the *didache,* the basis for discipleship, and *kerygma,* the basis for evangelism.

Evangelism and Discipleship: The Relationship

The last verse in Acts tells us that Paul was "preaching the kingdom of God" *(kerygma)* and "teaching concerning the Lord Jesus Christ" *(didache)* and that this was done with all openness and unhindered (Acts 28:31). The blending of *kerygma* and *didache* in the work of the New Testament church leads us to conclude evangelism and discipleship go together. These two facets of Christian ministry are inseparable in the New Testament. Therefore, two truths are self-evident. Evangelism that does not result in discipleship is not evangelism, and discipleship that does not result is evangelism is not discipleship.

We expect a salvation experience to lead to a changed life that gives evidence of the commitment. When persons accept Christ as their Lord and Savior, they will become active and involved in the work of the church. The fruit of evangelism is discipleship.

The relationship of *kerygma* and *didache* confirms that the receiving of Jesus' teachings resulted in evangelism. Today there is a proliferation of discipleship materials especially related to youth ministry. A major test of these materials must be, Does their proper usage result in evangelism? We never find a group in the New Testament who met together for only fun and fellowship. A weekly discipleship group that never gets involved in evangelism is not doing discipleship.

Christians are not to become fat on spiritual food and do nothing. The goal of discipleship is to help disciples know how to share the truth they have found. We are wrong when we assume persons have to receive many years of training before they can be involved in evangelism. More often than not, new Christians share freely the work of God in their lives. Discipleship without evangelism is not discipleship.

Youth ministry in general needs to be involved in evangelism and discipleship. There is a relationship between the two. Weak evangelism results in weak discipleship, and weak discipleship results in weak evangelism. The job is to blend both evangelism and discipleship together. This is the task of youth ministry.

Notes

1. William Barclay, *The Acts of the Apostles*, (London: SCM Press Ltd., 1953), p. 48.

2. T. C. Smith, "Acts," *Broadman Bible Commentary*, Clifton J. Allen, gen. ed. (Nashville: Broadman Press, 1970), 10:34.

3. Frank Stagg, *The Book of Acts*, (Nashville: Broadman Press, 1955), p. 58.

4. Ibid., p. 143.

5. C. H. Dodd, *The Apostolic Preaching*, (London: Hooder and Stoughton Limited, 1936), pp. 38-43.

6. C. S. C. Williams, *The Acts of the Apostles*, (New York: Harper and Row Publishers, 1951), pp. 41-42.

7. G. Campbell Morgan, *The Acts of the Apostles*, (New York: Fleming H. Revell Company, 1924), p. 60.

8. Barclay, pp. 21-22.

9. R. R. Williams, *The Acts of the Apostles*, (London: SCM Press Ltd., 1953), pp. 46-47.

10. Stagg, pp. 249-250.

11. Robert A. Bartels, *Kerygma or Gospel Tradition: Which Came First?* (Minneapolis: Augsburg Publishing House, 1961), p. 97.

12. Bernard Ramm, *Protestant Christian Evidences*, (Chicago: Moody Press, 1957), p. 192.

13. James S. Stewart, *Heralds of God*, (Michigan: Barker Book House, 1946), p. 199.

5
Youth Discipleship
and Basic Christian Disciplines
Bill Cox

On numerous occasions I have asked youth groups this question: What is a disciple? The most frequent response is: A disciple is a follower of Jesus. If we start with that simplified understanding of discipleship, we need to consider what it means to follow Jesus.

What does it mean to follow anyone? If we follow someone, we go where he or she goes and do what he or she does. Following Jesus, therefore, would involve going where He went and doing what He did.

Some people may argue that a disciple is a "learner" and put an emphasis on knowing and comprehending the various teachings of Jesus. Jesus repeatedly reprimanded those who had knowledge but did not practice what they knew. In Matthew 5, 6, and 7, Jesus emphasized the importance of acting on His teachings in both a humble public way and in a private way. Failure to do so is accompanied by monumental results. "Every tree that does not bear good fruit is cut down and thrown into the fire. So then, you will know them by their fruits. Not every one who says to Me, 'Lord, Lord' will enter the kingdom of heaven; but he who does the will of My Father who is in heaven" (Matt. 7:19-21, NASB).

Therefore every one who hears these words of Mine, and acts upon them, may be compared to a wise man who built his house upon the rock. . . . And every one who hears these words of Mine, and does not act upon them, will be like a foolish man, who built his house upon the sand. And the rain descended, and the floods came, and the winds blew, and burst against that house; and it fell, and great was its fall (Matt. 7:24-27, NASB).

Jesus did not leave open an acceptable option of knowing His teachings but not abiding by them. His call to discipleship was, "Come, follow Me."

Those disciples who physically walked with Jesus were able to go where He went and do what He did in a firsthand way that is not possible for us roughly two thousand years later. The authority we have in knowing what Jesus did, and, thus, what we need to do, is the Bible. We gain much insight into our basic Christian disciplines by observing the example that Jesus set as recorded in Scripture.

Bible Study and Scripture Memorization

In fact, consistent study of Scripture is one of the first and foremost disciplines necessary for a follower of Christ. Jesus was a student of the Scriptures. As a youth, Jesus knew so much about the Scriptures that He amazed the religious leaders of His time (Luke 2:41-52). How did He know so much? By virtue of being God's unique Son, was the little baby Jesus born with all scriptural knowledge? Or did He have to study like the rest of us? Luke 2:52 says, "Jesus kept increasing in wisdom and stature, and in favor with God and men" (NASB). If He kept increasing in wisdom, then He must not have known it all in the manger. Jesus' wisdom must have grown as He diligently studied Scripture with the help of God's Spirit.

That knowledge of Scripture gave Jesus the ability to resist powerful temptation for forty days in the wilderness. Jesus responded to temptation by turning to appropriate scriptural guidance that He had committed to memory (Matt. 4:1-11; Luke 4:1-13).

Jesus also turned to Scripture to help determine His identity and mission in life. He recognized Himself as the Suffering Servant revealed in Isaiah 52:13 through 53:12. Jesus frequently quoted this and other Old Testament passages that gave Him direction for His life and ministry.

Jesus recognized that His life was a fulfillment of Scripture. He said,

> Do not think that I came to abolish the Law or the Prophets; I did not come to abolish, but to fulfill. For truly I say to you, until heaven and earth pass away, not the smallest letter or stroke shall pass away from the Law, until all is accomplished. Whoever then annuls one of the least of these commandments, and so teaches others, shall be called least in the kingdom of heaven; but whoever keeps and teaches them, he shall be called great in the kingdom of heaven (Matt. 5:17-19, NASB).

Jesus fulfilled the Law and the Prophets, and He used them as the basis for His teaching.

If youth are to consider themselves followers of Jesus, they must follow Him in Bible study. They certainly have similar needs that Bible study and Scripture memorization can help meet. Teenagers today are pounded by temptation as they live in very sophisticated wilderness. They need biblical direction to know how to resist. Most, at some time in their lives, grope for identity, purpose, and direction. The Bible offers insight into who they are and why they exist.

Paul advised his young friend Timothy to

> continue in the things you have learned and become convinced of, knowing from whom you have learned them; and that from childhood you have known the sacred writings which are able to give you the wisdom that leads to salvation through faith which is in Christ Jesus. All Scripture is inspired by God and profitable for teaching, for reproof, for correction, for training in righteousness; that the man of God may be adequate, equipped for every good work (2 Tim. 3:14-17, NASB).

Any attempt to be a disciple without a commitment to Bible study will result in inadequacy. Youth need the teaching, reproof, correction, and training of the Scriptures to be able to function properly. They need it to be equipped properly for service.

Following Jesus includes following Him in a commitment to Bible study and Scripture memorization.

Prayer

Jesus' prayer life was also recognized by His disciples as a key ingredient worth following. "It came about that while He was praying in a certain place, after He had finished, one of His disciples said to Him, 'Lord, teach us to pray just as John taught his disciples' " (Luke 11:1, NASB). Were the disciples interested in prayer just because John had taught his disciples to pray? Or was it because they recognized prayer as a source of power for everything Jesus did?

Throughout their time together, the disciples couldn't help but notice the high priority that Jesus placed on prayer. Even when multitudes were waiting to hear Him speak, Jesus took time to go out in a boat away from the crowd in order to pray. He went up into the mountains to pray. When facing the major crisis of His life, He spent all night praying in the garden.

If Jesus Christ, the Son of God, saw such a great need for prayer, how can any of us possibly think that we don't need to be disciplined in prayer? Jesus taught much about prayer. Prayer goes far beyond the simple concepts in which prayer is reduced to memorized prose, a shopping list, or a cry for help only in times of trouble.

Youth need to learn not only the "If you ask Me anything in My name, I will do it" of John 14:14 but also the "Abide in Me, and I in you" of John 15:4 (NASB). They need to have scheduled time alone with God in private settings (Matt. 6:6), but they also need to grow in their ability to pray without ceasing (1 Thess. 5:17). A maturing prayer life involves not only a verticle relationship with God but also horizontal relationships with others, as we even pray for those who persecute us (Matt. 5:44) and forgive those who have offended us (Mark 11:25).

Being a disciple includes being disciplined in a consistent commitment to prayer.

Sharing Faith

In John 13:34-35 Jesus said, "A new commandment I give to you, that you love one another, even as I have loved you, that you also love one another. By this all men will know that you are My disciples, if you have love for one another" (NASB).

The disciplines of Bible study and prayer are mainly private matters that others do not normally see us doing. Jesus didn't say that people would watch us pray or read Scripture and say, "That must be a Christian disciple. He's sitting there with his eyes closed and just finished reading that cowhide-covered Book." What people will notice is the result of those disciplines. The most important expression of our discipleship should be love. People will know we are Jesus' disciples when we love each other. That goes far beyond just holding hands and getting our minimum daily requirement of hugs.

For starters, the love of a disciple leads to making other disciples. "Go therefore and make disciples of all the nations, baptizing them in the name of the Father and the Son and the Holy Spirit, teaching them to observe all that I commanded you" (Matt. 28:19-20, NASB). In this passage Jesus commanded us to lead other people to Him and then to nurture, equip, and train them so that they can do the same for someone else. We need to be making disciples because of obedience to Him and because of a genuine love for others.

The same love that Jesus has for us should motivate us to care about the eternal destinations of people around us. Jesus literally gave His life so that people might have salvation. If we are Jesus' followers, going where He went, doing what He did, motivated by His love, and obedient to His commands, we must develop a conscious discipline in evangelism. If we don't love enough to actively care whether people go to heaven or hell, we aren't loving enough to be recognized as disciples of Jesus.

Jesus provided the means to salvation, but He was also concerned about the everyday here-and-now needs of people. He ministered to the sick, blind, lame, hungry, lonely, hurting, outcast, downtrodden, and poor. If we're following Him, we must be concerned about the same needs.

In fact, according to Matthew 25:31-46, Jesus expects His disciples to care about the needs of others. He said to the extent we care or don't care about others, we care or don't care about Him. If our discipline doesn't include activities like feeding the hungry, giving drink to the thirsty, caring for strangers, clothing those without clothes, and visiting people who are sick or in prison, we might not find ourselves on Jesus' discipleship list no matter what kind of notebook we carry.

Churchmanship/Encouragement

Another aspect of loving one another involves our fellowship with other Christians, and the best place for this fellowship is in your church. Mention fellowship to most church youth and immediately they think of going over to someone's house for refreshments after Sunday evening services. Or maybe covered-dish suppers in the fellowship hall come to mind. Christian fellowship must go deeper than little pimento cheese sandwiches and cold fried chicken. There's nothing wrong with Christians gathering for fun and social activity; but at other times, more is needed.

> Therefore encourage one another, and build up one another, just as you also are doing. But we request of you, brethren, that you appreciate those who diligently labor among you, and have charge over you in the Lord and give you instruction, and that you esteem them very highly in love because of their work. Live in peace with one another. And we urge you, brethren, admonish the unruly, encourage the fainthearted, help the weak, be patient with all men. See that no one repays another with evil for evil, but always seek after that which is good for one another and for all men (NASB).

First Thessalonians 5:11-15 deepens the responsibilities and privileges of Christian fellowship rather significantly.

Believers need to provide encouragement and to build up one another. Very often teenagers get caught up in the opposite. As they struggle with their own low self-esteem, the natural tendency is often to tear someone else down. Subconsciously youth think, *If I can step on someone else and put them down, that will somehow elevate me and make me feel higher up the ladder.* Discipline in the ministry of encouragement is important.

Paul called special attention to the ongoing need to encourage, respect, and appreciate Christian leaders. The casualty rate of youth leaders is sad. Many more still on the field of service could be classified as walking wounded. Youth leadership forces would be greatly bolstered if more youth honored Paul's request.

Paul further reminded us that real Christian fellowship includes the often difficult responsibility of admonishing the unruly. Real love risks misunderstanding and rejection by trying to help one who has strayed get back on the right path. Patience and the ability to seek good, even for those who've done you wrong, are further ingredients of maturing Christian fellowship.

Anyone serious about doing what He did must realize Jesus' holiness. Jesus said to be holy as He was. In fact, in Matthew 5:48 Jesus said, "Therefore you are to be perfect, as your heavenly Father is perfect" (NASB). How can we be perfect and holy when Romans 3:23 reminds us that all have sinned and fallen short of the glory of God? We need to be consistently disciplined in 1 John 1:9: "If we confess our sins, He is faithful and righteous to forgive us our sins and to cleanse us from all unrighteousness" (NASB).

In our anything-goes society where the only creed seems to be "If it feels good—do it," it's not easy for youth to live holy lives. Most don't try to live by biblical standards. Christian youth face the great temptation to fit in and not appear too different. Genuine commitment to follow Jesus in living a pure life is necessary. Most believers only come close with tremendous discipline. This discipline overlaps greatly with ones we've already discussed. Without commitment to Bible study, believers have difficulty knowing how to fully live right. Apart from fervent prayer, believers don't have enough strength to do what they know they should do. The assignment becomes harder if there is no Christian fellowship to provide encouragement, admonishment, and accountability.

Jesus as Example

Jesus set the example of having pure thoughts, words, and actions.

If youth are not following Him in trying to do the same, can they really claim to be Jesus' followers?

We could go on and on with specific things that Jesus did that His disciples ought also be doing, but as John 21:25 reminds us: "There are also many other things which Jesus did, which if they were written in detail, I suppose that even the world itself would not contain the books which were written" (NASB).

Following Jesus means not only doing what He did but also going where He went. That premise could be approached in several ways. We could talk about the specific places that Jesus went, whether it was to minister, to worship, to pray, to retreat, or whatever. Much of that is included in our thinking about what Jesus did.

But Jesus did go one place that merits special consideration. He went to the cross. In a very real way, anyone who wants to follow Christ must also go to the cross. Discipleship must begin at the cross as the basis for relationship with Jesus Christ. Following Jesus to the cross must also be a daily discipline. "He was saying to them all, 'If anyone wishes to come after Me, let him deny himself, and take up his cross daily, and follow Me. For whoever wishes to save his life shall lose it, but whoever loses his life for My sake, he is the one who will save it'" (Luke 9:23-24, NASB).

The disciplines of Bible study, Scripture memorization, prayer, holy living, and loving others through evangelism, social concern, and Christian fellowship are vital. But these practices alone fall short of what is expected of a disciple. Jesus said following Him must be accompanied by a discipline of daily denial. Selfishness and desires apart from God's will must be put to death each day. Jesus said that we find the real life He wants for us only when we lay down our lives in this way. No amount of other discipline will compensate for refusal to do this.

In Summary

How important are basic Christian disciplines to youth discipleship? The question is almost ludicrous. That's like asking, How important is hydrogen to water? Without the disciplines Christ established, there is no discipleship.

In my early years of youth ministry, the materials and models for small-group discipleship were not nearly as available as they are now. Youth ministers and volunteer leaders developed their own materials and basically tried to follow the example of Jesus. Our approach included training leaders to each lead a small group of youth who were willing to make the commitment to grow spiritually. We had three main objectives, which I mention in reverse importance.

Our third priority was the teaching material that we wrote. Too often the material becomes the key focus. Youth can get the idea that our objective is to simply go through a determined amount of lessons. If the material becomes the priority, no matter how good it is, discipleship runs the risk of being reduced to a program rather than a lifelong commitment to Jesus Christ.

The second most important concern in our strategy was to put youth into a relationship with a trained, growing leader and counselor who could say along with Paul: "Be imitators of me, just as I also am of Christ" (1 Cor. 11:1, NASB). Youth often need to see someone else following Christ to be able to do so themselves.

The top priority was to use the material and leaders as a means of helping youth become grounded in their own basic Christian disciplines such as we've just discussed. We knew that we could not keep everybody in discipleship groups forever. We knew that they would eventually lose or cast aside their notebooks. We knew that as they grew up and moved on in life we'd lost contact with many of them.

But we also knew that if we could help them become disciplined in a few key areas, they'd have the tools and the means to remain lifelong disciples, truly committed to following Jesus Christ.

6
Discipleship Training for All Youth
Curt Bradford

For some time discipleship training has been targeted only to those youth who are *ready*. By *ready* is meant, "ready to make the commitment required for deeper spiritual growth." Ready to spend time alone in quiet time, ready to study the Scriptures, ready to witness, ready to "get serious" with God, and ready "to be discipled." To be discipled began to sound like an initiation rite for the "really committed" youth, while the average Christian teenager was content with Bible study through the Sunday School, practical Christian training through the Church Training, and missions sensitivity through the missions organizations. In an organization founded by one who taught greatness equaled being last, a spiritual elite was formed: Super Christians. The implication was that either you *really loved Jesus* and were a member of a special discipleship group, or you were just *saved* and participating in "plain ole church programs."

While there is definitely a place for the "deeper seeker," little discipleship training appears to be available for the youth who has not decided to be a notebook disciple. What training is done with this youth, this less than totally committed youth?

We must first deal with the idea of commitment. Youth are at varying levels of commitment in every youth group. Some youth have not made the commitment to salvation. They are exploring their options, so to speak, and the commitment may be more to the "family" known as the youth group than to Christianity or Christ.

Some youth received Christ years ago but have chosen to be nominal members only. The reasons for this level of commitment need to be explored and dealt with if we are to continue discipling persons at any age.

At one level of commitment, youth participate in every offering of the church. They are involved in Sunday School, Church Training, choir, missions organizations, choir tours, and recreational activities. They even visit a prospect or two when the youth director asks, but they do not want to be part of a special discipleship group that meets on Tuesday afternoon and does a notebook.

A fourth level of commitment is often referred to as the "totally committed youth." This youth is just like involved youth except that he or she does a notebook study and weekday study groups. This youth is rare and often a key leader in the group.

My premise for this chapter is that the discipleship programs prevalent today are targeted toward the youth who is involved in all church programs, including weekday groups that keep notebooks. Based on Jesus' model, discipleship training should be offered to all youth, regardless of their commitment level. Now, what training is currently done for youth with other levels of commitment?

For the most part we do nothing. We offer membership in our deeper Christian groups and if they choose not to join, we pray for them and hope they will soon come around and become part of the group. If this system is propagated, then the only discipled persons in the local church are those people with a notebook or those who are meeting in small groups with a study leader at some time other than Sunday.

The most serious problem with this system of discipleship is its narrow scope. Thousands, perhaps millions, of disciples of Jesus of Nazareth have never owned a notebook, met on Tuesday afternoon, or memorized Scripture. These disciples should receive discipleship training at the commitment level to which they have moved and in a way conducive to their spiritual growth.

The serious youth ministry coordinator will be developing ways to offer discipleship training for those youth who have made the commitment required for such indepth courses as DiscipleYouth, as well as developing ways to offer discipleship training to the other youth who are part of the program. This means ethical, doctrinal, and relational teachings for youth who are not part of a notebook study with small-group meetings. This also means that *some* training will be available for the youth who has not yet made the commitment to trust Christ. This form of discipleship training has evangelism as its thrust.

As a youth educator one cannot withhold the content from those who have not committed to in-depth study. This means a plan for discipleship training for all youth must be developed.

Does this concept hold when examined biblically?

Biblical Basis

To find specific words from the mouth of Jesus that either propose or oppose the idea of discipleship training for all youth is futile. Jesus, indeed, made statements that could be construed to be in opposition to the idea, such as "count the cost." But these statements were intended to serve as teaching instruments for those who had decided to follow Him.

In the "count the cost" passage (Luke 14:28-30), Jesus revealed the depth of commitment He requires for a total life to be changed by God for God's use. Many want to be His, but unchanged. The entrance into the kingdom of God is a free gift of God, but growth as a disciple costs us our lives. Jesus said to count the cost before opting to become a deeper disciple. Perhaps many youth have counted the cost and decided not to grow deeper in Christ. In so doing, they have not rejected Jesus, but the deeper life. They still need to receive as much discipleship training as can be provided at their level of commitment. The youth leader's prayer should always be for the Holy Spirit to convict the youth of their need for growth.

Jesus spent time with His disciples. The verse that introduces the Sermon on the Mount (Matt. 5:1) seems to indicate only the special group called "the twelve" were present. The conclusion of chapter 7, however, reveals the amazement of the crowds at the teaching of Jesus. Clearly these teachings (which were for the most part ethical, doctrinal, and practical, that is, discipleship) were spoken for those willing to hear.

Based on this passage, Jesus seems to have offered instructions on how to follow Him to those who had not yet decided to follow Him. This may have been His way of enabling would-be disciples to count the cost. By sharing the demands of total commitment, Jesus allowed persons to decide about their commitment and to involve mental processes, as well as emotional and physical, in the decision.

In another important episode, Jesus taught the multitudes about seed planting (Mark 4:1-20). Later when alone with a smaller band of followers, He responded to their request for more explanation. The spiritual truth given to the multitudes required more in-depth treatment with the chosen disciples.

This event communicates the truth that the content of the teachings of Jesus are like seed planted, but the actual produce is brought about through (and only through) the enlightenment of God. Jesus enlightened the twelve concerning these teachings. The Holy Spirit enlightens the believer today as to the deeper meanings of the teachings of Jesus. This enlightenment also is a free gift from God given to His children at their request.

The implication of this truth is that the discipler is responsible for communicating Jesus' life and teachings through model, words, and witness. The disciple has the responsibility and the only authority to cause these teachings to result in a life more deeply committed to God.

This is not to suggest a mystical hocus-pocus-type discipleship but rather to accentuate the role of the discipler in communicating the teachings, the role of the disciple in responding, and the role of the Holy Spirit as the enabler to the deeper life.

The role of youth educator-discipler is one of seed sowing. Since Jesus referred to the seed being scattered everywhere, the youth at all levels of commitment are entitled to learn of Jesus and then respond.

Two events in Jesus' life involving His family demonstrate another biblical thought concerning discipleship for all youth: One may attest to the messiahship of Jesus, hear His teachings, choose not to obey, and later come to a fuller understanding. Early in Jesus' ministry, his own people (Mark 3:31) came to rescue the Son and Brother who appeared to have lost His senses. The family came to rescue the member who was spending Himself on others. His brothers did not at this point believe in Him (John 7:5).

Most likely Mary never forgot the visit by the angel Gabriel, the visit by Wise Men, or the divine conception of her firstborn child. She no doubt attested to the special divine nature of Jesus; but during this event, she wanted to stop Him from His teachings and mission to bring her boy home.

Later we discover Mary at the foot of the cross, at the gravesite on Easter morning, and in the upper room awaiting the Holy Spirit. We also find Jesus' brother James as the leader of the church in Jerusalem. What could have happened to these two individuals? Obviously they became aware that Jesus was God incarnate. When this dawned upon their consciousness, the teachings of Jesus took on new meaning. Their belief (salvation) had now become commitment (discipleship).

In summary, this is the biblical evidence: (1) Jesus had followers (disciples) of varying degrees of commitment; (2) Jesus offered discipleship-type training (that is, ethical teachings, relational teaching, doctrinal teaching) to all persons who were in His audience, regardless of their commitment level, even scoffers and doubters; (3) the Holy Spirit is the agent who functions as a catalyst to the teachings of Jesus to bring about changed lives, and (4) Jesus had believers in Him who were not followers of His teachings. Based on these findings, I conclude that discipleship training was offered to any who were in the presence of Jesus. The idea of discipleship training being only for a special group is not biblically sound. The propogation of such an idea could result in the clergy and super Christians being all who could be called disciples. The youth who has trusted Jesus as Savior but comes only to Sunday School is a disciple. The impact of Christ on that life is minimal due to the lack of commitment, but the youth is still a disciple.

Two solutions come to mind: (1) preach, teach, and pray that this youth will join a deeper discipleship group or (2) offer discipleship training whenever this youth is present, praying for the Holy Spirit to cause change to come about.

How do we provide discipleship training outside the context of the separate group meetings with a notebook?

Here are three basic points to discipleship: (1) learning the teachings of Jesus, (2) relating those teachings to all of life, and (3) living that life. The facilitation of youth discipleship will need methodologies that enable the youth at varying levels of commitment to hear, relate, and live.

In the educational process, this will involve several approaches: content transmittal, problem solving (application), trial and error, modeling, on-the-job training, apprenticeship, team work, special projects, specific needs meeting, and assignments.

In many situations, unfortunately, content transmittal has become the dominant mode of discipleship training. Leaders have the misconception that if one knows the right thing to do, one will do it. So great spans of time are spent dispensing information to the minds of fifteen-year-olds in hope of discipling them.

While we do have a set of doctrinal truths to be transmitted to every new generation, this was never intended to be the primary method of discipleship. Jesus lived a life which included teachings. Jesus' primary occupation was not speaking when crowds gathered but teaching through His life as well as His words. Therefore, programs must communicate discipleship content to youth with varying degrees of commitment.

In the Southern Baptist Convention, the program is known as Church Training. In the Youth Church Training program, discipleship topics are transmitted through various teaching techniques in a group setting involving all youth. This approach is much the same as Jesus' dealing with large crowds. The content remains the same as other approaches, but the methodology varies. For example, in the teaching about the seed, Jesus instructed the crowds as well as the twelve. He transmitted a truth about the kingdom of God to two different groups, using an example the hearers could comprehend: a sower. The large group heard a story. The smaller group heard a deeper explanation of the story. The large group received the doctrinal teaching, while the smaller group received that teaching plus understanding. In a Church Training context, discipleship areas are communicated to all youth present. Response is up to the individual youth.

In dealing with the large group in discipleship, one will be communicating age-group truths that some will immediately appropriate, others will learn, others will forget, and others will bury until moved by the Holy Spirit to rediscover.

Each discipleship program should have a way to transmit discipleship teachings to a large group of individuals with varying levels of commitment.

In this context, because we are dealing with youth, we need to be sure to use creative teaching techniques that demonstrate these truths are not to be buried but applied. Case studies, problem solving, and youth as leaders are examples of teaching techniques in large-group situations that cause deeper learning to take place.

In the large group context, the leader will need to function as a facilitator to small-group activities rather than as a lecturer with information to give. This is an excellent place to use deeper-discipleship group members as facilitators, building up their leadership skills. Discipleship training for all youth must involve small-group work, or it will become merely another church activity to be endured.

Some youth will require more time and more explanation. Often these youth have made a conscious decision to follow Christ more closely. They have decided not only to *know* the teachings of Jesus but to join His mission. These youth will need a group leader who can spend intimate time with each youth in more intensive training.

Normally such youth want more understanding of God's message in Christ and want to probe their faith to the depth. In short, they might be called part of the twelve.

This youth is a member of the larger group of youth, so she must be involved in the large-group learning activities. Because the youth is spending more time learning about Christ (as a result of a greater commitment), this youth functions as a leader in the large-group setting. The youth could also be a small-group leader or facilitator.

Youth who have expressed this level of commitment will require some basic tools to spiritual growth that can be used at their discretion. These tools include quiet time, prayer, Bible study, ministry, and witness. Resources which equip youth to pursue these activities on their own are available. A good example is Disciple-Youth, which trains youth in basic Christian disciplines.

Another type of youth discipleship must be pursued in addition to the large group (the five thousand or the multitudes) and the small group (the twelve). This is the individual discipleship relationship that the youth leader has with one or two youth in the group who seem to attach themselves to the leader.

The inner circle (Peter, James, and John) is the model for this group. Some youth have an intense need to go beyond the five thousand or the twelve and want to go as deeply as possible in a relationship with Christ. These individuals require one-to-one training and time.

The youth leader will need to interact with these individuals as concerns and needs arise. The youth leader will need to be more transparent with these individuals and take more risks in trusting. These individuals do not simply want to know about Jesus. They want to know *Him*. For the most part, they see Him in the lives of other Christians, most notably the youth leader.

The discipleship training for these youth is more complex. The youth leader will need to be open to dialogue, debate, and even hostility due to the proximity created by the closer relationship. But these youth will be able to share in relationships with others on an intimate basis because of the youth leader's model. In this type of discipleship training, the primary method is time spent modeling.

The methodologies vary with the groups, but basically training should be for the large group, for the small group, and for the individual youth.

When does this training take place?

In Southern Baptist churches, a program exists to have the large-group discipleship program. It is the Church Training program and in most churches takes place on Sunday evenings. DiscipleLife Celebration is a format in which youth choir, snack supper, discipleship training, worship, and fellowship can be combined and coordinated to train youth in discipleship.

The meeting of the small groups (the twelve) for discipleship could be afternoons after school, prior to visitation, or weekends, depending on the schedule of the youth and the leader in the group. This time should allow for some on-the-job training, however, since this group will require more than content transmittal. The meeting time should be flexible enough to allow this type training.

The individual time should be as needs arise and at "teachable moments." One cannot always structure when the young disciple will want to discuss the in-depth things of God. For the one-to-one training, *flexibility* and *availability* are the key words.

Where is the training offered?

The large-group training should be offered in a church setting or camp setting. The youth who have made a minimal commitment to discipleship will probably not be open to church activities other than Sunday School, worship, or Church Training, so use the programs available to accomplish the mission.

The small-group training could take place in homes or the church. The setting needs to be such that it is not another church meeting but something more. Homes are ideal for these meetings of the twelve.

One-to-one training by its nature takes place in churches, homes, schools, or other places as needs arise.

Conclusion

The youth disciple is the one who has made a commitment to Christ as Savior and Lord. There are varying levels of commitment to growth, so discipleship training should reflect these degrees and provide appropriate training for all youth who have made the commitment to Christ rather than the select few who have elected to study a notebook.

7
Stages of Youth Discipleship Development
Martha Jo Glazner

Discipleship development is the task and vocation of every Christian. The process is not unique to youth. Yet, between ages twelve through seventeen, or in grades seven through twelve, adolescents are experiencing changes in their lives that make certain aspects of spiritual growth particularly significant. Decisions persons make during adolescence affect the rest of their lives. These are decisions youth must make for themselves. Parents, teachers, and church leaders cannot make them for youth. Those who try will find the experience unhealthy for themselves and for the youth.

What is the process of discipleship development? It is the process of Christian growth, of modeling one's life after the life-style of Jesus Christ, of nurturing one's soul with Jesus' teachings from God's Word. Discipleship development has both inward and outward dimensions. In communion with God, the disciple discerns who he or she is and what God wants from him or her. The disciple acts on that knowledge in the world. Through practice, the person develops skills in ministry, leadership, and witness.

Discipleship development with youth has both present and future dimensions. Adolescent disciples are struggling with change daily. Their bodies are changing dramatically, their emotions fluctuate between excitement and depression, and their minds marvel at the wonder of *why*. They are asking a million questions, some verbally and some unvoiced. As they struggle with questions such as "What is God like?" and "Why am I like I am?" they are forcing themselves to decide what they believe and how those beliefs will shape their lives.

In this section, we will look at ways in which discipleship development and adolescent developmental tasks parallel each other. The outline for the chapter is based on the stages of discipleship development listed by the Youth Section of the Church Training Department, The Sunday School Board of the Southern Baptist Convention. These stages are experienced by persons of any age when they make a faith commitment to Christ. The point is to show how the development of a personal faith and a life-style of discipleship can be experienced during adolescence.

Stages of discipleship development will not be completed at age seventeen, nor will they happen for all people in the sequence listed. The process continues throughout a person's life. Concerning the stages of life, and of discipleship, John Hendrix wrote:

> All of life can be seen as a stretching or a shrinking back. Each stage of life has an inward propulsion, a powerful thrust from within, to move on toward maturity in Christ. At the same time there is a tendency to shrink back, a force running counter to propulsion, filled with dread and fear of growth, and a seeming paralysis in moving forward.
> . . .
> Growth from one stage to the next is not automatic and not directly related to age. Biological maturation, chronological age, psychological development, mental age, and life story are all factors that affect the readiness to move from one stage of development to another.[1]

The First Stage: Commitment

Christian discipleship begins with acceptance of Christ and a profession of that faith to God and the Christian community. Some twelve-year-olds have made a profession of faith when they were younger. Others will make that commitment during adolescence.

The Process of Faith Commitment

Commitment of life to Christ begins with a recognition of need. Youth who have been in church all their lives may not realize their need for making a profession of faith. Church leaders need to help youth see their need for God, for the Holy Spirit's presence in their lives to help them in coping with life's problems. Youth need to understand the difference in being good and being Christian.

God wants a personal relationship with every human being He created. He will not force Himself upon us. He gives us the choice of life with Him now and in the future or life separated from Him. To choose life with God, the individual must believe that God loves him, that He expressed His love by giving His only Son, and that Jesus triumphed over death (John 3:16; Rom. 10:9-10). This powerful belief is more than factual; it becomes deeply rooted in the heart, mind, and soul. Upon confession of need, declaration of belief, and commitment of self to God, God's presence in the form of the Holy Spirit dwells within.

This commitment, with the presence and power of the Holy Spirit, expresses itself in a new way of life, lived under Christ's lordship. This means modeling one's life-style after that of Jesus Christ, seeking God's guidance in daily decisions, communicating regularly with God through prayer and Bible study, and assertively acting on trust and faith in God. The refrain "Trust and obey" expresses well this life-style.

The Significance of Youth's Faith Commitment

Whether a Christian commitment was made at an earlier age or whether it is made during junior or senior high, youth need to understand their experience and its impact on all their lives. Because of their increasing ability to think abstractly, youth have the capacity to understand more than they did at an earlier age. They are in the process of moving from concrete intellectual operations to formal thinking. This means that, in terms of their religious experience, symbols of faith take on deeper meaning. Youth can begin to realize the meaning of baptism's symbolism and that commitment to Christ as Lord means applying His teachings to every area of their lives. Because they are beginning to see themselves related to a past and future, their concept of faith takes on future dimensions. They begin to calculate how their faith impacts their plans for the future.

Leading Youth to Commitment

The primary commitment of every individual is to God. Other commitments follow and are based on that foundational commitment. Because youth experience the faith commitment to God at various times, periodically it must be emphasized and reaffirmed during the youth years. As one youth verbalizes what the commitment means, others are challenged to think about their own faith. Because youth need a person on whom they can depend, who cares for them, they will respond to these qualities of God. Emphasis on God's love and care for each individual can go a long way toward leading youth to commitment. Openness and willingness to listen and to share personal experiences of relationship to God can facilitate youth's trust in God. "The adolescent's religious hunger is for a God who knows, accepts and confirms the self deeply, and who serves as an infinite guarantor of the self with its forming myth of personal identity and faith."[2]

The Second Stage: Community

Youth's quest for identity and for belonging can be explored and experienced in Christian community. Jesus' disciples experienced community as a band of twelve learners who accompanied and assisted Jesus in ministry. The disciples' commitment was translated into supportive relationships with each other. Today the church offers a caring community where youth can feel safe to explore their personal identity and affirm that identity in relationships.

Defining Christian Community

"Christians are in community because they are in the Spirit. They speak a common language, a spiritual talk about Jesus, the Word of God. Christians are in community because they share a common experience, the experience of acknowledging Jesus Christ as Savior."[3] Stories of the early church in the Book of Acts help us to see how

Christians in the church can experience community. They had "all things in common" (Acts 2:44, RSV). They sold their possessions to give to those who were in need. They worshiped together, ate together, and welcomed new Christians to join them. (See Acts 2:44-47; 4:31-35.) Christians in community affirm, support, and encourage one another. The Greek word for Christian fellowship, *koinonia,* characterizes Christian community as it is experienced in the church. With persons of all ages interacting, the church is like a family; it is a "family of faith."

Youth Growing in Community

What better place/people can youth find for testing their concepts of self, of God, of life, than a community of Christ's people who want the best for one another. Followers of Christ seek to help each other and to reach out in love and acceptance. Because youth are experiencing rapid physical changes, they are often shy and embarassed. The church can be a mirror to reflect positive feelings of self. Those feelings can be nurtured in an atmosphere of love, even when youth are struggling and fluctuating emotionally. In Christian community, youth can see God's love modeled by caring adults. They can be led to move out of their self-centeredness to empathize with other people and give themselves in loving service.

Leading Youth to Experience Community

Church leaders can show youth by example what Christian community is. Leaders' genuine friendliness, acceptance, and attitude of openness will be perceived immediately by youth. Youth can be trained/equipped to extend these same qualities to peers.

Leaders can help youth to see that church membership involves both giving and receiving. Church members are responsible for themselves and for one another and for contributing to the good of the whole. As individuals grow in the faith, seeking to follow Christ, they cause the "growth of the body for the building up of itself in love" (Eph. 4:16, NASB). Christians in the church nurture and encourage one another to grow in the faith.

Small groups in the church provide a vehicle for youth's experience of Christian community. As individuals share their fears, hopes, and dreams, trust grows and participants are strengthened for daily living. They are equipped to give themselves in loving service and to act on the strength of their convictions.

The Third Stage: Calling

God's call to individuals takes various forms. Basically, God's call is an inner sense of a special connection, communication, with God which endows the believer with responsibility. His first call to each person is the call to salvation. As the faith commitment grows within the individual, there is the feeling that God has a special purpose for one's life. This is true for every Christian. Some individuals feel that God calls them to use their talents and abilities in a Christian vocation or career. Youth who are growing in their faith and are experiencing new adventures at church and at school are beginning to envision what their futures might hold. They need to come to grips with the concept of Christian calling and how it impacts their decisions now and in the future.

Confirming the Sense of Call

Youth need both internal and external confirmation of their calling from God. The inner confirmation comes as the Holy Spirit works within the individual. As youth begin to know themselves—to discover their talents, interests, and abilities—they see that God has given them a special combination that is unique to them. Through Bible study, they see how God called biblical persons, such as Abraham, Moses, and Jeremiah, and how they fulfilled their calling. Prayers can become avenues of talking and listening to God, hammering out frustrations and fears and turning them into dreams and creative actions.

External confirmation of calling comes as persons significant to youth call on them for specific tasks and then identify the special gifts youth have exhibited in completing the tasks. A sincere compliment from a significant person gives the youth affirmation and

strengthens their commitment to give themselves to God. Quite often, the sense of God's will being done in one's life comes in retro-
spect. When things fall in place or work together, Christians have the
sense that God is at work in their lives. Because they have not yet
lived long enough, youth do not have this advantage. Yet, they will
begin to see little things fall into place. Their responsibility now is
to be obedient and responsive to God in the use of their gifts and in
the decisions they make.

Youth Acting in Response to the Call

Younger youth need to nurture their sense of God's purpose for
their lives by exploring all the things in which they have interest and
ability. They need to focus on general goals for their lives, to live in
communion with God, and to develop their gifts. Older youth will
begin to refine their understanding of God's call, as they accept their
limitations and as they channel their gifts toward specific options.
They, through more active involvement in school and church activities, have begun to see what possibilities are open for them in terms
of careers and educational opportunities.

Leaders Facilitating Youth's Response

Intense religious feelings are characteristic of youth. They are
looking for a cause to which they can give themselves. Retreats,
camps, and mission trips can give youth opportunities to dream, pray,
and listen to God. Through active participation in mission projects,
youth can try out their skills and clarify their sense of direction
concerning careers. Inventories and studies about talents and gifts
can provide new visions and confirm earlier ones. Leaders who are
available to youth can share insights, affirm youth's hunches, and
help them clarify questions and concerns.

The Fourth Stage: Covenant

The word *covenant* in the Christian context refers to God's relationship with His people. God acted to bring humanity into relationship
with Him. That act of redemption was renewed several times in the

Old Testament and sealed through the death and resurrection of Jesus. God has always remained faithful to His covenant with humanity, but human beings have not always been faithful in keeping their part. We see this in the nation of Israel and in people today. Based on God's bond of love with us and our faithfulness to that covenant, we live and relate in God's world.

Covenant and Life

Life's deepest relationships are sealed with covenants, two-way promises/pledges of love, faithfulness, and devotion. God gave us the pattern for mature relationships when He established and continually renewed His covenant to remain faithful in loving and caring for His creation. We find many examples of such relationships with God in the Bible—Abraham, Moses, Jeremiah, and many others. God gave these people tasks and promised to support them in carrying out those tasks. Throughout the Bible, we see evidence of God's faithful support. His bond of love is eternal.

Youth's Readiness for Covenant

By accepting Christ and committing their lives to Him, youth have accepted the responsibility of living in covenant relationship with God. Though they may not have realized it at the time, by the ninth or tenth grade, external pressures to conform to society's demands may cause them to question or rebel against their earlier faith commitment. Going through such a process can bring forth a stronger commitment and deeper relationship with God. Some youth may have to search and try out some other things before they take hold of the deeper commitment. To come to a point of volition, of personal will, regarding their relationship with God can open youth to new vistas of lasting commitment.

Leading Youth to Affirm Their Covenant

Sometimes in the church, youth respond to intense religious experience by rededicating their lives or even making a new commitment of faith, feeling that their first experience was not valid.

Sometimes youth compare their experiences with those of other persons and doubt that their earlier commitments were real. Leaders need not to be alarmed by such feelings or confessions. They are a natural part of growing in faith. Only the individual and God know the validity of the first experience. Once a genuine commitment is made, God remains faithful to the individual. Everyone needs to evaluate and reconfirm commitments periodically. Those commitments are strengthened in the process. Leaders are encouragers, affirmers, and nurturers who transmit God's love to youth.

On the basis of their covenant with God, youth covenant with other persons to establish relationships of enduring quality. Some have specific time limits, such as a group which meets for a specific time and purpose. Church members covenant together to support the life and work of the church. As youth become more involved in church life, they help to shape the church's covenant.

The Fifth Stage: Competency

Competency refers to the disciple's having the knowledge, skills, and spirituality to do God's work effectively in the world. Being competent as a disciple of Christ is to be equipped for service in God's kingdom. The process of becoming a competent servant of God is a lifelong task. Christians mature in the faith through study, reflection, motivation, and experience. Jesus taught the disciples to be fruitful, to produce much fruit—fruit that was good in quality. Not only does this include telling the gospel story and leading others to make a commitment to Christ but it also involves helping the new Christian to grow in Christ.

Competent in Knowledge

Competent disciples need to understand the basic truths of the Christian faith, to wrestle with theological issues enough to be firmly established in what they believe. Not all can be understood; some things will always remain mysteries. God is so much greater than human beings can comprehend. Through junior and senior high school, youth need to have opportunities to openly and honestly examine concepts about God, Jesus, the Bible, the Holy Spirit, church, prayer, and other aspects of Christian faith. They need to become acquainted with persons in Christian history, their causes, struggles, and accomplishments. They need to examine ethical issues from a Christian perspective and come to some conclusions about their stance. Youth need exposure to the life and operation of the church so that they will be equipped for leadership, both now and in the future.

Competent in Skills

If disciples are to produce the fruit which Jesus called for, they must develop ministering and witnessing skills. Some basic concepts and procedures can be introduced in a group learning experience, but practice through apprenticeship and actual experience gives opportunity for lasting growth and development. Some youth will back away from the personal exposure involved in such experiences, but others will be challenged. Some youth may find their gifts are more naturally suited to ministering to persons with special needs. Church leaders can train them to carry out their ministry with compassion. Other youth may find their skills lie more in the area of performance, such as music and drama. Others may find expression for their faith in art or creative writing. Every person is not competent in every area. Christian disciples, however, do seek to incorporate witness and ministry with their other skills.

Spiritual Competence

In Philippians 3:13-14, Paul wrote: "Brethren, I do not regard myself as having laid hold of it yet; but one thing I do: forgetting what lies behind and reaching forward to what lies ahead, I press on toward the goal for the prize of the upward call of God in Christ Jesus" (NASB). An abiding relationship with Christ that is nurtured through regular quiet times of prayer, Bible study, meditation, and journal keeping will nourish youth's relationship with God. Not only is the relationship sustained in these quiet times but God also walks with the individual throughout the day, and mundane chores some-

times become beautiful discoveries. The commonplace can become a
sanctuary for prayer and celebration. To see the world through God's
eyes is to make each moment and each day a new beginning.

Guiding Youth Toward Competence

Adults in the church need to show youth that they believe in them
and trust them. Such an attitude shows when youth are entrusted
with responsibility and leadership. Youth Week, mission trips, and
worship leadership can become memorable for the youth and for the
church as a whole. Being with the youth in preparation, behind the
scenes in support, and in evaluating after the experience will provide
the help that will strengthen youth and facilitate their growth toward
competence.

The Sixth Stage: Commissioning

Before Jesus left the disciples, He commissioned them to go and
take the good news of the gospel to people everywhere. In giving
them these instructions, He promised that He would be with them,
giving them the strength and power they needed to carry out the task.
Not only were the disciples to lead people to Christ but also they
were to baptize them and teach them to observe God's guidelines for
living. This same commission is in effect for Jesus' disciples today. All
Christians are disciples, and all Christians are to share God's love.
Christ's commission takes many forms. People live out the commission through their vocations. For some this may mean going to distant lands to invest their lives. For some this may mean teaching
school or working in a factory. Whatever Christian disciples do,
wherever they go, they carry the love of Christ to a world that is
hungry for acceptance, affirmation, and fellowship.

Commissioning Youth

Participating in church life during junior and senior high school,
youth have gained a growing consciousness of what Christ's commission means to them personally. They have set some goals for their
lives and have plans, by the time they are seniors, for fulfilling those

goals. Many will depart from family and church to prepare for a career, or to enter a job they have chosen. Whatever their plans, life after high school will be different. Church and home will never be quite the same. Church leaders need to prepare youth and give them their blessing as they go.

Preparing for Departure

Church leaders need to communicate to youth that God's call to His disciples is not easy. God equips them for the task and promises to be with them. Many times, God will come to them through other Christians. The location or vocation may change several times as they feel God working in their lives. God's call is dynamic; it is nourished through quiet moments with God and through personal growth experiences in churches and campus organizations. Practical experiences, such as summer mission work and teaching or leading church groups, can help youth continue to clarify God's purpose for their lives. Leaders need to encourage youth to invest themselves in church life wherever they may be. The experience can be mutually rewarding—for the church and for the youth. A community of faith can be a source of encouragement and provide youth a "home away from home."

Going with God's Blessing

A church can affirm youth's sense of personal worth and seal the bond they have in Christ by expressing to youth upon graduation from high school their confidence and good wishes. Such expressions can be made through a special worship service, personal contacts, and continual communication after the youth leaves home. When youth return to church, they need to be welcomed with open arms and made to feel that they still belong. Special times at Christmas and other holidays will reinforce the support of the church and encourage the youth to maintain church affiliation.

The Stages Continue

As stated earlier, most of these stages of discipleship happen throughout life. What I have done here is present a way of bringing together the developmental processes of junior high and senior high youth with discipleship development. I hope you will see how this can provide a handle for integrating the activities and experiences of youth ministry toward specific goals and objectives. Much more can be added to this basic outline at every stage. Youth ministers and coordinators can add to, adapt, and use this as a planning tool for a six-year strategy of youth ministry.

Notes

1. John D. Hendrix, "Discipleship Development," *equipping youth*, October 1985, p. 8.
2. James W. Fowler, *Stages of Faith* (San Francisco: Harper and Row, Publishers, 1981), p. 153.
3. Bill Hendricks, "Biblical Discipleship: Community," *equipping youth*, April 1986, p. 4.

8

The Role of Church Program Organizations in Youth Discipleship Development

Wayne Jenkins

What is the most important function of the church? With this hackneyed question, we begin our investigation of the role of the church as a discipling influence in the lives of youth.

The answer to the question often rests upon the answerers' bias. This bias may be shaped by how one came to know and follow the Lord Jesus Christ; it may depend upon background, personality, scriptural interpretation, theological bent, doctrinal understanding, training, tradition, occupation, indifference, ignorance, preference, desire, or zeal. For example, preachers proclaim the priority of preaching, Christian educators hold high the educational function of the church, and evangelists believe that winning souls to Jesus is the truest calling of the church.

Musicians extol the virtue of the choir and the graded music program; the mission-minded broadcast the missionary mandate, emphasizing that all Christians are missionaries; pastoral ministers counsel all Christians to be ministers. Likewise, of course, are those in the church who dwell on discipleship, insisting that everyone should practice the daily disciplines of discipleship and consistently disciple others as followers of Jesus Christ.

Who would argue with any of these spiritual priorities? Each function of the church is important and scriptural. However, the sum total of the maturing Christian life is not any one element of the faith. It is not only Bible study, although Bible study is important. It is not only music ministry, although Christian music is an assest to the individual and corporate Christian experience. Mission education and mission action are not all there is to the Christian faith, neither are preaching, witnessing, ministering, or worshiping.

The answering of the-most-important-function question is at the heart of the program organizations of the local church. Program organizations (Pastoral Ministries, Bible Teaching, Discipleship Training, Missionary Education, and Church Music Development) as defined by Robert Orr in his book *Being God's People* exist to ensure that all of the vital functions of the church are performed effectively. Balance is essential to positive spiritual growth and results from the proper operation of each of the program organizations. These program organizations are dedicated to the accomplishing of the following tasks in the church and in its individual members:

Unless the various programs of the church are ministering at their full potential, youth and other members of the congregation may grow into deformed spiritual beings. When development fails in any portion of one's spiritual character, one becomes very strong in certain areas of faith and very weak in others, making a powerful spiritual life impossible.

Some Christian youth grow up through outstanding Bible study programs. The youth attend Bible study on Sunday morning, Sunday night, Wednesday night, and even on a week night. They go on Bible study retreats. Some also study the Bible at school. These youth know what the Bible says, they know where to find needed verses, they have several passages committed to memory, but they may miss the mark in their ethical obedience to the commands and calling of Jesus Christ. Mission and ministry may be the farthest thing from their minds. Doctrinally they may be babes. Their leadership skills may be dormant.

Another common example of exclusiveness in spiritual development, is a church that places undisputed priority on choir. "If you're not in the youth choir, you're really not in." In such a church, youth choir meets on Sunday night, eliminating other types of training at that hour and excluding youth who are not choir inclined. Youth choir sponsors trips, retreats, socials, and other outings, making other

ORGANIZING THE WORK OF A NEW TESTAMENT CHURCH

Pastoral Ministries Program	Bible Teaching Program	Church Training Program	Woman's Missionary Union Program	Brotherhood Program	Music Ministry Program
● Lead the church in the accomplishment of its mission	● Reach persons for Bible study	● Reach persons for discipleship training	● Teach missions	● Teach missions	● Provide musical experiences in congregational services
● Proclaim the gospel to believers and unbelievers	● Teach the Bible	● Orient new church members for responsible church membership	● Engage in mission action and personal witnessing	● Engage in missions activities	● Provide church music education
● Care for the church's members and other persons in the community	● Witness to persons about Christ and lead persons into church membership	● Equip church members for discipleship and personal ministry	● Support missions	● Pray for and give to missions	● Lead the church to witness and minister through music
	● Minister to persons in need	● Teach Christian theology and Baptist doctrine, Christian eithics, Christian history, and churh polity and organization	● Interpret and undergird the work of the church and the denomination	● Develop personal ministry	● Assist church programs in providing training in music skills and in consultation about music equipment
	● Lead members to worship	● Train church leaders for ministry		● Interpret and undergird the work of the church and the denomination	
	● Interpret and undergrid the work of the church and the denomiation	● Interpret and undergird the work of the church and the denomination			● Interpret and undergird the work of the church and the denomination

program organizations struggle in its shadow and producing for non-choir youth an even harder struggle to belong.

Youth in a youth choir-dominated youth ministry gain much in the area of worship, service through music, discipline, musical training, motivation, and perhaps vocational guidance. A beautiful spirit of belonging develops for those who participate.

But, as in the case of the exclusive Bible study program, the music ministry as the only stay for youth's spiritual development in the church is not sufficient. No matter how outstanding the youth choir program is, it is still a youth choir program. It is not designed to meet the comprehensive spiritual needs of youth. It, like Bible study, satisfies some vital spiritual needs, but not all.

We are pendulum people. Rather than achieving balance and comprehensiveness, we tend to rush headlong after one goal to the neglect of all others. After we have pursued that particular ideal for a while (maybe even for a generation or more), we then look around to notice that we are only serving one purpose in the lives of youth. We are shocked to behold their weakness in other crucial areas of development. After a while, one certain deficiency screams at us long enough that we are convinced that something needs to be done, so we begin to shift our priorities. We say things like, "Our youth know nothing about ____," or, "Why are the youth in our church so appallingly ____".

Suggestions begin coming to the youth leadership. Motions may be made in business sessions or committee meetings of the church. Low and behold, a new obsession is identified, and the church's youth ministry scampers after it.

Sadly, the concern of the change makers is not typically in the favor of comprehensiveness, but adjusted exclusiveness. Adjusted exclusiveness is never going to nurture able, strong, mature, godly disciples. It might, however, produce proficient specialists. But Jesus Christ did not command the polishing of a proficient specialist; He mandated the making of disciples (Matt. 28:19-20).

Basic to the American educational revolution of the late 1800s and early 1900s was the premise that education was the solution to all social ills. Educating the masses was to achieve a perfect society. An informed individual was expected to function with intelligence and honor.

This educational revolution was, thus, one of quantity. Everyone should be provided the opportunity of an education. In the early twentieth century, therefore, the societal obsession for America was educating the masses. Education was regarded as the answer, so a noble, effective, lasting campaign was launched and is now accomplished—everyone in the United States has an education available to them through the public school system, according to the law.

The success of the public school movement and the educational revolution can be evaluated by two criteria. Criteria number one: Did it educate the masses? Yes! Criteria number two: Did it transform humanity into crimeless, responsible, honorable, productive, moral citizens? No! Education for everyone brought sweeping changes in the United States, but it has not eliminated crime, corruption, destruction, immorality, decay, hatred, inequity, prejudice, selfishness, or immorality.

Educational revolutionaries expected too much from mass education. Education educates. It does not perfect society or the human condition.

In the 1960s, bombarded with religious and social issues and pressures, Protestant families began an overwhelming appeal for schools which would teach Christian values in a controlled Christian environment. This outcry became a major offensive, and private Christian schools sprang up in most school districts, especially in the southern United States.

Proponents of private Christian education noticed that public education had failed to transform lives. They were suspicious of secular influences, teaching values, and environment. They feared the unknown repercussions of the total racial desegregation of the public schools. So some retreat and some advance birthed the private Christian school phenomenon which is a major contingency today.

Deep in the conception of the private Christian school was the desire to transform lives, perhaps even the desire to transform society. Has it happened? Are the private Christian schools successful? Again, the judging must be done by at least two criteria. Criteria number one: Have private Christian schools achieved a controlled environment and program of education? Yes! Criteria number two: Have private Christian schools transformed lives and produced godly, moral people in a godly, moral environment? No!

Working with youth all over the country reveals to me that youth in private Christian schools are confronted with every kind of temptation and pressure that is present in the public school. Many youth resist the temptation in public and private schools. Many do not. Some youth in private Christian schools and in public schools are Christian. Some are not. Some youth in private Christian schools have problems related to alcohol, drugs, sex, hatred, intolerance, prejudice, jealousy, anger, self-esteem, parents, and so forth like those in public schools. The form, setting, and intensity may vary, but the difficulty is there just the same. Some youth deal successfully with these problems, some do not—in both public and private schools.

Although the full effect of private Christian schools will not be completely evident for another generation, education which is formed and practiced in the name of Christianity is no substitute for individual Christian faith, commitment, and devotion to Jesus Christ. Learning alone does not transform lives and society even when it is done in the most sterile of environments by the most-committed followers of the Way. The learner must become a follower, a disciple, of Jesus Christ.

Our educational ancestors and our educational contemporaries have failed to significantly Christianize society and individuals through the public or private classroom. "But," the book-learning loyalist may reply, "these are in the schools where so many other agenda are also at work. Certainly education in the church would be successful in transforming lives by the command and teaching of Jesus Christ."

Others thought so too. The religious education movement grew from the same basic suppositions as the educational revolution. Sunday Schools and other educational institutions of the church began to teach laypeople the truth of the Scripture. Paralleling educational revolutionary patterns and tenets, the leaders of the religious education movement assumed that the problems of the church and world would cease when every church member knew Bible, doctrine, theology, and other subjects vital to the faith.

The religious education movement of the late 1800s assumed that Christians could be taught to be responsible and mature followers of Jesus Christ. Believing that such areas of the Christian life as discipline, ethics, leadership, evangelism, spiritual development, and worship would grow in the proportion that an individual knew the Bible, religious educators marched into a new age for the church in which education became a priorty. The Sunday School became the most honored and popular function of the local church.

After generations of educating the Christian layperson, we evaluate the results and find that the religious education movement was unsuccessful in one key area. Discipleship!

Knowing the Bible is not enough to motivate the average Christian to live a godly life. Knowing that one should be evangelistic—even knowing how to witness—will not make a Christian boldly verbalize or demonstrate his faith. As it is not sufficient simply to know that God exists, knowledge is not the equivalent of or the route to powerful and elevated Christian living.

Knowledge, to be sure, is one of the aspects of the Christian life. For example, Christians need to know the message and truth of the Scriptures, Jesus Christ as Savior and Lord, about the power and promise of prayer, and about the fellowship and ministry of the church. But knowledge is a beginning. Beyond knowledge of the Bible is faith in and daily practice of God's Word. Beyond knowledge of Jesus Christ is acceptance, devotion, submission, and followship. Beyond the knowledge of prayer, likewise, is intercession and constant fellowship with God. Beyond knowledge of the church is spiritual growth, support, love, service, and obedience. Too many leaders and laypersons, however, treat knowledge as if it were the goal or the essence of true spirituality.

One who proposes that Bible study is the only discipline a Christian needs is being dangerously narrow in vision. One who elevates the Bible teaching program of the church as the key to a strong church and strong believers needs only to look at the spiritual aftermath of the 1950s. In the 1950's, Sunday School and church attendance were at their best. Where are those Bible students now? Where are their children and grandchildren? Where are those who were led by the scholars in those legendary Bible classes? Why is spiritual, social, and moral decay running rampant?

No! Education alone will not produce the kind of Christian follower which is silhouetted in Scripture. Then what will? Evangelism alone cannot. After great crusades, thunderous revivals, and powerful invitations, we wonder where those converts are who professed faith in Christ, recommitted their lives to Him, and were even baptized the second time because "the first one didn't take."

Neither can we rely merely on the church fellowship to sustain, nurture, and shape Christian believers. People get bored. Feelings get hurt. Moods change. Relationships burn out. Individuals move away. Pastors and staff members come and go or stay too long. None of the ways we have considered is a worthy approach to totally and permanently change the spiritual lives of youth.

Therefore, tenured youth leaders reviewed the fruit of their labor and found that youth who were active in high school youth groups gave in to all kinds of worldly pressures. The strongly spiritual youth seemed to be an exception even in thriving church youth groups.

When youth group members graduated from high school, little remained from all the hours spent with the youth group. Church attendance dropped. Commitments waned. Fellowship with God was sporatic at best. Christian ethics only served to impose a tinge of guilt on the morning after. The recreational/educational approach to youth ministry was not shaping lives in the image of Christ.

Consequently, in the mid 1970s, a discipleship re-awakening brought with it the strategies and the intent to change the trends of spiritual decline. Programs, agencies, and courses were developed to help Christians grow as disciples of Christ. Youth ministry was most strategically effected by the discipleship reawakening. Youth ministers began seeking ways to disciple teenagers. When investigating a program or study resources, youth ministers asked how that material would disciple members of their group. As they planned youth ministry, in general, the discipling quotient became primary. One-to-one discipling, small-group discipling, and large-group discipling was begun by church staff and volunteer leaders.

Discipleship, as officially defined by the Baptist Sunday School Board of the Southern Baptist Convention, is:

> "The Christian's lifelong commitment to the person, teaching, and spirit of Jesus Christ. Life under Jesus' Lordship involves progressive learning, growth in Christlikeness, application of biblical truth to every area of life, responsibility for sharing the Christian faith, and responsible church membership."[1]

Since education can only be expected to educate, evangelism only to evangelize, and so forth, we have to turn to a broader, balanced system of developing the spiritual lives of youth. The religious education movement was not enough. It was too narrow. It put expectations in the wrong places. It sought to bring changes that religious education could never broadly and generally accomplish.

The original religious education movement should have actually been a discipleship movement since discipleship shapes lives in the image of Jesus Christ through training, education, prayer, modeling, molding, missions, ministry, apprenticing, worshiping, evangelizing, counseling, preaching, loving, sharing, and disciplining. The problem with all the previous attacks on carnality is that they centered on one area of the Christian life or another and concentrated on effecting it as if changing that one area of life would change all the others.

Discipleship, on the other hand, is to effect the entire life. Everything a person is, does, and thinks is to be submitted to Jesus Christ. Discipleship is not one slice of life. It is an ingredient that blends into and characterizes every part of life.

Discipleship is not one isolated spiritual discipline but the orchestration of all personal spiritual disciplines to produce comprehensive growth, strength, service, and devotion to Christ. Neither is discipleship training a separate entity in youth ministry. On the contrary, discipleship training is like flour that is mixed throughout an entire loaf of bread. Discipleship training should be the goal in every area of youth ministry. Youth ministers need to disciple parents and leaders of youth, so youth can be discipled at home and in the program organizations by adults who are already following Christ as disciples.

Since discipleship training is not a separate responsibility of the church which is serviced at only one designated hour per week, all church staff and youth leaders are called to be disciplers. The pastor should be a discipler and so on. As discipleship is not one area of life but is the whole Christian life, discipling is not confined to any one segment of ministry.

Although the minister of youth, for example, has many varied tasks in working with teenagers, discipleship should be the objective of all tasks. That is, the objective of a retreat, a Bible study, a mission trip, a visitation, a youth emphasis, or whatever should be to disciple the youth involved. Ministers of youth should be disciplers.

Similarly, the minister of music or the youth choir director should set as his goal the discipling of youth rather than simply having a good choir rehearsal, a beautiful anthem, a wonderful choir tour, or a stirring solo. Ministers of music should be disciplers.

Rather, than setting preaching as the purpose or visiting as the purpose, discipleship should be the purpose or visiting as the purpose, discipleship should be the purpose, the aim, of all that the pastor does. Pastors should be disciplers.

Likewise, Sunday School teachers, mission education leaders, and Sunday night youth leaders should all be disciplers. Their aim should be to disciple teenagers through ministry, through missions, through witnessing, through outreach, through projects, through relationship, through role modeling, through encouragement, through discipline, and through fellowship.

How is discipling done across all program lines? The first way is to be a disciple of Jesus Christ yourself. Let Jesus be the Lord of your total life. Spend time with Him daily in worship, Bible study, meditation, and prayer. Make the most of group Bible study and worship by taking notes on meaningful parts of the session. Be involved in personal witness and ministry. In other words, be an example of discipleship.

The second way is to set discipling youth as your goal for each thing you do. Ask Jesus Christ to use the group time in His process of shaping lives in His image and bringing the youth to be submissive to His lordship. Dedicate all content and activities to serve this purpose.

The third way is to work as an individual disciple as well as a group disciple. Discipling is not either a group or an individual task. It is accomplished both in the group and individually. Through visits, cards, letters, and shared projects during the week, pick out certain youth at particular times of the year who will be the object of your intense attention. Train them as leaders. Show them how to witness and minister as they witness and minister with you. Allow them to learn to plan and to lead by planning and leading with you. Guide them in keeping a daily time alone with God by letting them share in your daily quiet time with God. Enable them to pray, read, and study the Bible, meditate on Scripture, memorize Scripture passages, and so forth as they do it with you.

Way number four is to encourage and exhort youth. Develop the kind of relationship that will allow this kind of open communication. Over a period of time and through various proofs of love, care, and reliability, win the right to be heard. Encourage characteristics, strengths, abilities, and calling which you perceive in youth. Caution youth about dangers, weaknesses, and difficulties you detect. Help them avoid or overcome these.

Way number five is to work in conjunction with parents and other youth leaders who are with the members of your group at other hours of the week. Work as a team with these parents and leaders, a team that is seeking the same discipleship goals in the same lives through the same Lord and Savior. No program organization or youth leader can effectively operate in isolation from the others.

The sixth way is to organize a discipleship organization for youth, perhaps on Sunday evening. This weekly group session would bring into focus all the discipleship experiences of the week and reinforce these. It and its leaders would serve as discipleship resources to all other youth leaders and to parents. The youth discipleship group would meet regularly to deal with topics vital to growing youth disciples, such as commitment, ethics, theology, doctrine, devotion, leadership development, and personal ministry. The format of these sessions would be similar to the traditional Wesley "class meetings" in which participation, facilitation, and enabling are essential. For Southern Baptists, the Youth Section, Church Training Department, Baptist Sunday School Board, Nashville, Tennessee, provides resources and organization for youth discipleship groups.

Way number seven is never to give up. Customize your discipleship to the age of the youth you are discipling. Seventh and eighth graders need to dwell on their salvation commitment to Christ, on self-esteem, and on the values and responsibilities of belonging to Jesus Christ and to His fellowship—the church and particularly the youth group. Ninth and tenth graders need to be reminded of those topics, but they can move on to becoming aware of their gifts, abilities, and personality in terms of how God can best use these throughout their lives. Likewise, ninth and tenth graders can begin understanding the priviledges and commands involved in relationship and daily fellowship with Jesus Christ. Eleventh and twelfth graders who have this kind of foundation are ready to develop their skills so they can fully serve and follow Jesus Christ. They begin to perceive themselves as equipped and sent out to minister in the name of Jesus Christ.

Successful discipling is a process. It is repetitive. It is progressive. You may only do one layer of discipling—perhaps the seventh grade layer—and someone else will follow you in the eighth grade layer, and so forth. Recall 1 Corinthians 3:6-8: "I planted, Apollos watered, but God was causing the growth. So then neither the one who plants nor the one who waters is anything, but God who causes the growth. Now he who plants and waters are one; but each will receive his own reward according to his own labor" (NASB).

Beware! Focus not on one aspect of discipleship to the exclusion of any others. That is easy, but dangerous. And keep telling yourself: "All youth and youth leaders are potential disciples of Jesus Christ." Go! Disciple youth!

Note

1. From *Church Base Design 1986 Update,* pp. II: 51. © Copyright 1986 The Sunday School Board of the Southern Baptist Convention. All rights reserved.

9
The Youth Minister
as an Equipper
Wes Black

The door clicked shut as Bryan breathed a long, depressed sigh. He slumped into the chair and looked at the youth ministry calendar on his desk. Plans needed to be made, and events needed to be scheduled.

Frustration, despair, and *disappointment* seemed to describe Bryan's feelings after a year of intense activity in the youth ministry of the church. He had worked as hard as possible to lead the youth in spiritual growth. Counseling, discipleship groups, one-to-one discipling, new Christian follow-up, and large-group seminars had been in his list of activities the past year. Still he felt the program was inadequate. Too much was left to be done. Too few people were involved. No one seemed to really care.

Bryan's feelings indicate common problems to youth ministers who seek to disciple youth but ignore the storehouse of gifts and energies available to them. The "Lone Ranger" model of discipling youth brings with it problems of loneliness, exclusiveness, narrowness, and selectivity.

However, there is a better way. Equipping adults who, in turn, touch the lives of youth in all areas of their lives leads to a broad, comprehensive ministry. The youth minister who multiplies his or her ministry by equipping others to disciple youth gains a depth that is impossible to achieve alone.

Why an Equipping Ministry?

There are at least two good reasons for an equipping approach to youth discipleship. First, the Bible strongly suggests it as the appropriate way to do ministry. Secondly, it is a practical necessity in today's youth ministry.

The Biblical Mandate

First Peter 2:9 is one of the most remarkable statements in the New Testament: "You are a chosen race, a royal priesthood, a holy nation, a people for God's own possession, that you may proclaim the excellencies of Him who called you out of darkness into His marvelous light" (NASB). In the Old Testament, only the members of the tribe of Levi could perform priestly duties. In the New Testament church, however, everyone has become a priest! All of God's children have the privileges and responsibilities of priests before God.

All Christians have been gifted with potential for service (1 Cor. 12:7). These spiritual gifts form the power and potential for doing the work of ministry (Eph. 4:12). For a youth minister to ignore this element of God's will for His church would be a tragic mistake and biblically unsound. The ministerial gifts, especially as seen in Ephesians 4:11-16, are given for equipping the saints (all believers) to do the work of ministry. It cannot be a one-person show.

The life and ministry of Jesus is also a model of equipping others for service. Matthew 10:1-15 is the record of Jesus instructing and sending out His twelve disciples. He recognized the benefit of working through others to do His ministry.

Luke 6:12-16 records the occasion when Jesus prayed and then called out the twelve disciples. They were an interesting bunch. He did not call only the scholars and well-to-do from Jerusalem. He used people from all walks of life, in every social strata, and even those who were social enemies with each other. He used the common, untrained followers to be channels for His ministry.

Finally, Paul instructed Timothy to equip others for ministry. "The things which you have heard from me in the presence of many witnesses, these entrust to faithful men, who will be able to teach others also" (2 Tim. 2:2, NASB).

A Practical Necessity

Today's youth ministry is much broader than the old style of simply providing fellowship activities after church on Sunday night. The needs of adolescents and their families in the latter part of the twentieth century is almost staggering. A "Coke and a joke" might have been sufficient to keep young people entertained in some by-gone era, although that approach never was spiritually adequate. Youth ministry must touch the lives of youth in all areas: socially, emotionally, physically, mentally, and spiritually.

Drug abuse, alcoholism, sexual pressures, suicide, sexual diseases, family breakdown, and an increasingly secular society are just a few of the issues facing youth today. Guiding youth in their spiritual decisions and growth is a tremendous challenge for today's youth leader.

The leadership of youth groups in the church also calls for multiple gifts and energies. Ongoing training groups, one-to-one discipleship, discipleship courses, short-term training, new Christian and new member training, discipleship seminars, and other discipleship events present an array of leadership needs that must be filled. One person cannot do all the leadership alone.

This is more than a job for one person. Even in the smallest church, youth need more than one adult role model in their discipleship growth. Leaders who relate to youth in Bible study, discipleship training, missions and music groups, and the church family at large need to be equipped in some facets of youth discipleship.

The youth minister who tries to do all this alone has a severe handicap. It is like trying to accomplish the mission of the church with both hands and feet tied. In fact, 1 Corinthians 12:12-27 gives the picture of the church as a body, with the members like different parts of the body. All parts are important and all parts need to be equipped for ministry.

Not all members are called or gifted for youth ministry. However, youth ministers should consider ways to equip those adults in leadership roles with youth, parents of youth, and youth themselves for the work of service.

Equipping Youth Leaders for Service

Adults volunteer to lead in the youth ministry of a church for a variety of reasons. Some reasons are appropriate, while other motives are less than ideal. The Holy Spirit gives gifts for the work of ministry, but those gifts may become abused in the midst of emotions, clashing personalities, and misguided priorities. An understanding of the reasons youth leaders serve will aid youth ministers in their equipping ministry.

Why do adults become involved in youth ministry? Many youth leaders serve out of a sense of call and a desire to serve God and their brothers and sisters in Christ. God calls volunteers into youth ministry as surely as He calls those who serve Him in paid positions.

Others serve out of a desire for self-fulfillment. There is a certain level of recognition from youth and other adult church members toward those who teach classes, sponsor trips, and counsel youth in their various activities. Some adults need the strokes and attention that come from being with younger people and being seen as a leader. The status and approval that comes from leadership with youth is a poor substitute for the sense of calling that comes only from God.

Finally, others serve out of a sense of guilt. This may come from a person's feelings that they have a debt to pay for their past sins. They may feel that their adolescent years were wasted and that this is a way to "pay back" for those misspent years. Still others serve because no one else will serve and they feel the church needs to provide leadership for their youth. Their service is a duty and responsibility rather than a grateful response to God's leadership in their lives.

A youth minister has the responsibility of equipping the saints for ministry, regardless of the reason for their service. There is room for counseling those who are serving for the wrong reason. Certainly this should be considered in enlisting any future youth leaders. However, the youth minister often must patiently serve with those who are searching for God's leadership in appropriate ways to serve Him. The following are some of the ways to equip youth leaders for service in youth ministry.

Informing and Encouraging

Communication is a monumental task. People are flooded with information on a daily basis. Newspapers, TV, radio, memos, personal conversations, telephones, bulk mail advertising, catalogues, and outdoor advertising scream for attention every waking moment. Some people tend to be overwhelmed and simply shut down the systems. Any new information has a difficult job of catching their attention.

A simple mailout from the youth minister's office will often be tossed into the wastepaper basket along with the other bulk mail of the day. An announcement from the pulpit on Sunday morning is likely to land on inattentive ears. A bulletin board in the hallway of the church must wrestle for attention along with the other billboards a person sees every day.

Youth ministers must be sensitive to the need for personal communications and not assume that one message will get through. News and information might need to be repeated in several forms—printed, spoken, visual—before it gets proper attention.

Computers are wonderful inventions. They provide the power and flexibility to handle complex jobs in more efficient ways. But computerized mailing lists are mixed blessings. A letter with a computer-generated mailing label is marked as an impersonal document. Many people are even becoming aware of the ability of computers to "personalize" letters from a mailing list.

Thank-you notes, birthday cards, memos to leaders, and announcements can all be prepared from one computerized list. However, a personal touch is needed if true equipping for ministry is to happen. High tech demands high touch. People still need the personal, sensitive element from those with whom they serve.

Youth leaders need a lot of encouragement. There are very few immediate rewards in youth ministry. The rewards often come years later when a young adult returns to thank a former youth leader for his/her patience and love in dealing with them as a youth. Youth ministers must provide the encouragement needed to keep going when the rewards are few. Encouragement is certainly a vital part of any equipping ministry.

Equipping by Supervising

Supervision is normally considered outside the work of the church. It is only for secular organizations with organizational charts, a chain of command, and power to hire and fire. But supervision can play an important role in equipping youth leaders for service.

When people work together, some flow of traffic and spirit of cooperation must exist. Certain understandings of responsibilities and expectations make it possible for people to work in various activities with different purposes, formats, and needs.

Youth Sunday School departments may meet in the same rooms used by Youth Church Training groups. A youth choir might rehearse there at another time. The simple job of sorting supplies and coordinating use of the facilities can become a barrier to fellowship if someone abuses the schedule. An Acteens group that schedules an overnight event the same night as the youth choir is supposed to be rehearsing for the next performance can expect some frustrated feelings among leaders.

Proper supervision can help avoid some of these logistical problems. Other problems between leaders, areas of responsibility, curriculum materials, and relationships with youth can also be avoided with good supervision. Supervision must be seen as a ministry of servanthood and support rather than a show of power and authority.

Co-Laboring in Ministry

The goal of equipping youth leaders for service is to lead them to be co-laborers in ministry. This involves several tasks that may be occurring simultaneously within any group of leaders.

Helping leaders to discover spiritual gifts is an exciting venture. Assigning responsibilities then becomes a joy for the youth minister and the leaders. When leaders realize the gifts and energies from God and find avenues for service, a supernatural joy grows and continually motivates them for service.

Training leaders in youth leadership skills and use of curriculum materials is another way to develop co-laborers in ministry. People become more equipped for ministry as they gain confidence in leading and guiding youth, handling discipline problems, understanding adolescents, and knowing how to plan and lead youth ministry. Knowledge of curriculum materials and resources gives youth leaders an arsenal of information as they disciple young people.

Building teamwork and goal setting is a third way to develop co-laborers in ministry. Youth leaders are more likely to be motivated and actively involved when they feel a sense of belonging and being needed. When adults feel like they are part of the team, that their ideas are important, and that their input is desired, they are more likely to look for additional ways to minister. The goals become "our" goals instead of "the youth minister's" goals and plans. Ministry becomes personal rather than an obligation.

Finally, the youth minister becomes a representative of a group of fellow laborers before the church. The youth minister serves as a representative of the church's youth ministry, working alongside many persons who touch the lives of youth with the good news in all areas of their lives.

Equipping Parents for Ministry

The parents of teenagers are critical factors in their behaviors, attitudes, and beliefs. Even though many parents feel frustrated in their efforts, research still shows that parents are the primary influence on the lives of their youth.

The Cradle of Theology

If youth leaders are to disciple youth in any life-changing ways, they must consider the impact of the home. The home is the cradle of a person's beliefs about God. The child's first and longest-lasting impressions about God, religion, faith, and Christian life-styles come from the home. The model of the parents' faith is a powerful influence on youth. A youth minister can influence youth toward Christ more effectively by equipping parents for their discipling role with their youth.

Parents can be an encouragement or a deterrent to their youths' discipleship growth. The youth minister may teach a youth to have a quiet time, minister to others in Jesus' name, share their testimony with friends, and be active in the fellowship of believers. But, if the parents of that youth never have a quiet time, never engage in ministry, never witness to lost friends, never share their faith with the family, and attend church infrequently, that youth will have many obstacles to overcome in spiritual growth.

Youth ministers need to recognize the impact of the home on the lives of teenagers and seek ways to minister to parents as well as youth. Youth do not exist in a vacuum. They each come from a family background which strongly flavors the way they relate to God.

Encouraging and Informing

Encouraging and informing parents about the church's youth ministry is one way to equip parents. Mailouts, church newsletters, a parent newsletter, parent meetings, bulletin boards, handouts, and telephone calls from youth leaders are just a few ways to inform parents. Personal contact, coffee breaks, lunch with parents, telephone calls, and informal fellowship with parents on Sunday mornings further inform them of the directions of youth ministry. Parent fellowships, parent/youth fellowships, and parent/leader fellowships serve as encouragement to parents of teenagers.

Training in Parenting Skills

Training in parenting skills is another way to equip parents for their discipling role. Offering parent seminars, panel discussions, guest speakers, and parent dialogue sessions will help parents who are struggling for answers in raising their teenagers. A youth minister would benefit greatly by making available good parenting books, periodicals for parents of teenagers, and brochures for parents.

Equipping Parents in Discipleship

A third way to equip parents is by equipping them for discipleship. Many parents would love to sit down with their families for Bible study or family worship, but they feel inadequate or just do not know how to get started. Along with encouragement to begin these activities, youth ministers should provide practical help in how to have a personal quiet time, how to lead a family Bible study or worship, and how to guide teenagers in spiritual decision making.

These suggestions should be taken in light of the overall program of discipleship in a church. Parents are part of the church's ministry to adults and should not be seen as an isolated slice of the body of the church. Youth ministers can work closely with those who plan and lead adult discipleship as well as offering specific guidance in discipleship as it relates to youth ministry.

Strengthening Families

Strengthening family units is a fourth way to equip parents for their discipling role. Plan parent/youth activities where parents and their teenagers can relax, laugh, and enjoy being with each other. Take into consideration the demands on family schedules and budgets in planning any youth activity. Look for ways to bring families together rather than planning for ways to keep them apart.

Use Parents in Youth Ministry

Finally, use parents as sponsors and counselors in youth ministry activities. Most parents have a built-in understanding of the demands and stresses facing youth of today. Many parents can relate well to other youth and make excellent camp counselors, sponsors for fellowships and trips, coaches for teams, and so forth. Most parents would rather have communication than confrontation with their youth.

Equipping Youth as Equippers

Youth are the best channels for reaching other youth for Christ. They serve either as a good model of a Christian young person or they discredit all that is taught in church. Any youth ministry must look for ways to equip youth who will pass on the things they have heard and seen.

Provide Well-Balanced Discipleship Program

A well-balanced youth discipleship program is perhaps the best way to equip youth for their discipling roles. Ongoing training on a weekly basis, for all youth, providing broad-based discipleship training is a necessity. Youth need a stable, consistent group they can turn to for acceptance and guidance during their teenage years. Short-term studies to meet special needs and interests, one-to-one training for personal help, and occasional seminars can augment the ongoing discipleship in the weekly groups that meet on Sunday nights. Discipleship courses and events should be offered to provide equipping in the skills of life-style discipleship.

Provide Atmosphere for Spiritual Growth

An atmosphere for spiritual growth is a second way to equip youth for ministry. Youth must have an environment conducive to spiritual growth if they are to mature as disciples. A sense of mission in the work of God sets the church apart from other entertainment media and is the only way a church can compete with the world's attractions in reaching and discipling youth today.

Provide a Caring, Supportive Youth Group

Third, a caring, supportive youth group helps equip youth for their discipling tasks. A sense of belonging and acceptance frees youth to become all God wants them to become. Youth do not have to have a lot of friends to feel accepted, but they must have at least one. A youth minister can aid in this struggle by helping the youth group to be open and loving rather than selective and snobbish.

Challenge Youth to Develop Gifts

To equip youth as equippers also demands that youth ministers challenge youth to develop God-given gifts and talents. Christian young people have gifts of the Spirit and can be involved in the work of ministry. Youth leaders should guide and encourage youth to discover their gifts and strive to become all God wants them to become as Christian young people.

Adopt the Barnabas Model of Discipling.

Finally, Christian youth can become disciplers of other youth by following the Barnabas model. Barnabas was the one who first took the new convert Paul by the hand and encouraged him to become a leader for Christ. Barnabas also encouraged young John Mark, even when he failed on the first missionary journey (Acts 13:13). Barnabas's encouragement resulted in John Mark becoming "useful" for service (see 2 Tim. 4:11). Youth can be encouragers for other youth who are young Christians. They can share with them as they walk along their journeys of discipleship and equip them for ministry.

Youth ministry is an exciting journey of discipleship. Equipping youth leaders, parents, and youth for discipleship will multiply the youth discipleship efforts and successes. It will also bring with it a deep sense of joy as many people find avenues of service in the kingdom of God.

10
The Importance of Modeling in Youth Discipleship Development
Chuck Gartman

"What you do speaks so loudly I cannot hear what you are saying" is the crux of this chapter. Allowing youth to see that what we talk about really works is the only validating evidence that can be defended in our lives. The Fellowship of Christian Athletes' motto is: "If you're going to talk the talk, then you have to walk the walk." That needs to be our motto as youth leaders as well. True, grace must operate in our lives, but we must never forget that we have a responsibility to show youth how the Christian life works on a daily basis.

Many coaches can tell or draw on the chalkboard ways that players can do better in their given positions. The best coaches seem to be the ones who are able to demonstrate the techniques about which they speak. However, it is not imperative that they be able to actually do what they desire of their players. While coaches may not absolutely have to be able to demonstrate the various methods of play, persons who intend to lead youth in the way of discipleship do not really have a choice about whether they should be able to demonstrate their concepts. As leaders, we must demonstrate or model the principles of discipleship in our lives.

Character and actions are very difficult, if not impossible, to separate. However, for the sake of organization and study, I want to divide the two. The first part of this chapter will deal with the personal characteristics of an adequate model. The second part will deal with some practical ways in which those character traits can be demonstrated in a tangible way to the youth whom we are leading. Following those two aspects of modeling, I will deal with some programming to help us in our modeling. Finally, I will touch on some problems that may arise in our seeking to be models to our youth.

Personal

Galatians 5:22-23 in *The New International Version* reads like this: "The fruit of the Spirit is love, joy, peace, patience, kindness, goodness, faithfulness, gentleness, and self-control. Against such things there is no law."

In the previous section of this chapter in Galatians, the description is given of the person who is controlled by the sinful nature. The source of that character is clear. It is from the inside—the part of a person that is controlled by the lower nature—that evil characteristics come. The acts are called sins. This means that a person really wants his own way more than he wants God's way. The description, here, is of the inward character of the person who is controlled by the sinful nature.

On the other hand, the two verses under consideration describe the character of the person who is under the control of the Holy Spirit. Listed are nine characteristics or personal character traits that are derived from the relationship of the believer to the Spirit of Jesus Christ Himself. Now, if a person wants to be a model of what youth will follow in discipleship, he must allow the Holy Spirit to so control his life that these characteristics will be evident in his life. The following are brief descriptions of the various personal traits that ought to be modeled by every believer in general but by disciplers, in particular.

Love

Romans 5:8 describes what love is really like. "God demonstrates His own love for us in this: While we were still sinners, Christ died for us" (NIV). True love accepts people just as they are ("While we were still sinners."), then it offers itself to meet the needs of others ("Christ died for us.") "This is neither shallow sentiment nor reciprocated benevolence. . . . its finest embodiment is in Jesus Christ."[1]

To be a model of discipleship, one must love in this manner. It will come from the depth of a person's character.

Joy

"Joy is two faceted in its expression. It is the gift of the Spirit that becomes a condition of the heart which is confident of its relationship to Christ—a forgiven sinner accepted by God's grace with the living Christ as daily companion. On the other hand, joy becomes the expression of celebration which empowers us to be Christian. Joy makes us strong, produces energy. . . . Joy cannot be self-created. . . . its only source is obedience."[2] The discipler who has a daily personal relationship with the Savior will exhibit this quality of life, naturally.

Peace

Peace is not a quality that indicates only an absence of conflict. It is the calm assurance that God is in control no matter what may come our way as Christians. For Christians, this quality of life is demonstrated in being willing to face life realistically instead of trying to escape from it.

Patience

The best description of patience is a "godly putting up with." "The great church father and preacher Chrysostom said that it is the grace of the man who could revenge himself and who does not."[3] This is not an easy trait to have. Modeling for our learners will require some discipline on our part to allow the Holy Spirit to produce patience in our lives.

Kindness

"The whole idea of the word [kindness] is a goodness which is kind."[4] "The yoke of Christ does not chafe or gall; it fits, it is easy. Does that not suggest a style of relationship, being with another in the way that Christ is with us, making the way of the other easier because we are *yoked* with them?"[5] What better description could there be of a person who wants to lead youth in the way of disciple-ship!

Goodness

Goodness is a balance word. While kindness is gentle and sweet, *goodness* is a strong word that demands accountability. The same word is used in the way in which Jesus cleansed the Temple of the money changers. As demonstrators of the character of Christ, we must have balance in our lives—kindness as well as strong goodness. Both are necessary.

Faithfulness

"In this context it [*faithfulness*] denotes the quality of trustworthi-ness or fidelity."[6] The word refers to reliability. How often we as disciplers desire that our students be reliable when we are not relia-ble. This a convicting word.

Gentleness

"The word [*gentleness*] conotes gentle strength."[7] "The meek [or gentle] person is the person who knows his or her strength, but submits that strength to Christ in a ministry of love and caring for others."[8] The person who is gentle is also teachable. We are to be not only teachers in our discipling but also continual learners.

Self-control

"It [*self-control*] describes the inner strength by which a man takes hold of himself, refusing to be swept along by errant desires or impulses. It is essential to freedom from the tyranny of the flesh."[9] Without this characteristic all of our teaching will be of little value. Allowing God to be in charge of our lives is what is meant by this quality.

We cannot possess these qualities of personal character without a vital relationship with Christ. However, let me reiterate that it is not an option in being a discipler to have an ongoing personal relation-ship with the Savior. It is an absolute necessity.

Practical

While having these qualities of character in our lives is important, how we live our lives, how those qualities "flesh themselves out," is equally important. Being a model to youth as we seek to disciple them requires that they are able to observe in us some consistency in how we live out our own lives.

Paul identified some ways disciplers can show that their Christianity works. First Corinthians 11:1 says, "Follow my example, as I follow the example of Christ" (NIV). The key to this verse is found in latter part, which indicates that the source of Paul's life was Christ Himself. Believers were to imitate Paul because he was imitating Christ. Philippians 4:9 ought to be a watch word for those of us who are trying to be models for youth in discipleship: "Whatever you have learned or received or heard from me, or seen in me—put it into practice. And the God of peace will be with you" (NIV). Paul's confidence was that he had lived his life in such a way that he could call attention to it without fear of someone pointing out his failures. He was a living example of the quality of person that he wanted his disciples to be. And the same should be true of us.

Here are some areas where we can model our faith to our fellow learners—disciples.

Personal Devotional Life

To me nothing is more important than having a high quality of life with God on a personal basis. The time to develop this has been called "quiet time," "daily time alone with God," or "daily devotional time." What we call it is not nearly as important as that we do it. In *DiscipleYouth*, the notebook for discipleship published by The Sunday School Board of the Southern Baptist Convention, the compilers, Clyde Hall and Joe Ford, identify three reasons a person should have a quiet time. (1) "A quiet time is a way of maintaining your fellowship with God." Keeping the lines of communication open with God will allow us as disciplers to have quality fellowship with the Lord. (2) "A quiet time is a way of building spiritual strength." No person is exempt from difficulties. People need additional strength to cope with the everyday hassles of living. The leader of youth is no exception. Staying in touch with God allows a person to build up a supply of strength and power to adequately deal with difficulties. (3) "A quiet time is a way of becoming more sensitive to God's leadership."[10] Discovering and following God's will for our lives is a process that takes daily communication with God to understand and do. Leaders who want to successfully lead youth in discipleship need to be able to discern God's leadership too. A fourth reason for quiet time is particularly important for the purpose of this chapter. The reason is summed up in this statement, "You can't lead someone in a direction that you yourself are not going." Leading youth to a deeper relationship with the Lord will require that we as leaders be on the same road. For us to hope that we can lead them in the proper direction without being on the same road is a pipe dream. It just won't happen. We will only be able to lead them as far as we have gone ourselves.

Faithful Worship

Hebrews 10:25 says, "Let us not give up meeting together, as some are in the habit of doing, but let us encourage one another—and all the more as you see the Day approaching" (NIV). Many of us tend to excuse our absence from worship by saying that we have a lot to do administratively. Though we may be busy, busyness is not a reason to neglect worship. Adequately modeling our faith in front of our youth necessitates our being faithful to worship, even as we ask them to be faithful.

Fellowship

As youth leaders we often feel that we must spend all our time relating to youth. Nothing could be further from the truth. As adults, we must also have Christian fellowship with adults. We will not be adequately fed and stretched unless we do. If we fail to have proper relationships with fellow Christian adults, we will likely burn out in trying to lead our youth to have fellowship.

Bible Study

There must be a time in our lives when we are studying God's Word for some other reason than just to teach it to youth. I believe we can get insight as we study to teach our youth, but I also believe that we must study the Bible for ourselves as well, with no thought of what we can teach from our study. We need to be fed personally from God's Word, for our own benefit, just as much as we need to study it in order to teach youth from it.

Sharing Our Faith

This may be the most difficult subject discussed in this chapter. We tend to share God's truth only with the youth we are leading. But adults in our lives need to hear our witness as much as any youth we may tell. One person I know has said that if we have no lost friends we need to get some. As professional staff members this is very difficult. Our natural inclination is to try to share our faith only with those who have visited our churches or who have expressed interest in the gospel because we are staff people. Our neighbors and community members also need to hear our concern for their spiritual lives not just because we are paid staff people but because we care genuinely about them.

Family

I do not want to put youth leaders in a fishbowl any more than we already are, but very few things carry more weight in today's world than what we do with our families. Modeling for youth what a quality family is like is next to impossible. Yet the principles of that kind of family need to be constantly in front of youth. If you are married, you need to treat your spouse with the kind of respect due a Christian mate. We do not need to pretend that we have no problems because, if we are honest, we have as many or more than other people. However, we need to keep uppermost in our minds that our mates are to be a priority in our lives. If you are a parent, you need to be the very best parent you can be. If you are the parent of a teenager, the task of modeling is even greater, but it is still of supreme importance. With divorce, broken families, and blended families on the rise, youth leaders need to live lives in such a way that youth can see that the Christian home works. It is not without problems, but there are solutions to those problems in Christ Jesus.

Quality of Life

Quality of life is a little more difficult to deal with, but I want to mention it because, as we seek to be models of the Christian faith this aspect is significant. The Sermon on the Mount will give some foundation, particularly Matthew 6:25,31-32:

> "Therefore, I tell you, do not worry about your life, what you will eat or drink; or about your body, what you will wear. Is not life more important than food, and the body more important than clothes? . . . So do not worry, saying, 'What shall we eat?' or 'What shall we drink?' or 'What shall we wear?' For the pagans run after all these things, and your heavenly Father knows that you need them. But seek first his kingdom and his righteousness, and all these things will be given to you as well" (NIV).

Our feelings about material things will be evident in how we live our lives in front of people. We all know that money and what it can buy is important, but we also know that it ought not to be *the* priority of our lives. Making God's kingdom a priority in our lives takes a great deal of effort at times, but the dividends will be worth the price. Being a tither of all that God has given us is not something we want to continually talk about, but being the kind of people who tithe is important. We will be hard pressed to teach that principle to others if we fail to practice it. What we do with the rest of our material possessions needs to be in line with what the Father would have us do as well.

Along the same lines is how we spend our time. Youth are very observant and will make assumptions about our use of time. We must be careful to allow them to see that our time is a gift from God as well as our money. If we are constantly using our time for our own pleasure and benefit, we won't be able to discuss with any degree of credibility that God has a plan for our time too.

And finally, we must be careful that we use the abilities that God has given us for God's purposes and His glory. Paul said, "Just as each of us has one body with many members, and these members do not all have the same function, so in Christ we who are many form one body, and each member belongs to all the others. We have different gifts, according to the grace given us" (Rom. 12:4, NIV). The utilization of our God-given gifts and talents is imperative if we are to be the kind of models that God desires.

In all these areas—material possessions, time, and abilities—we need to keep in mind our own goals. Youth need to realize that our goals in life are worthy and not just self-seeking. If mediocrity is our goal, that will be evident to any observant youth. On the other hand, if excellence is our goal, then they will be able to discern that as well. The primary motivating factor, though, is the seeking of God's kingdom first.

Temperament

Temperament is, also, a somewhat difficult subject with which to deal. It is a principle with practical ramifications. It relates to some of the character qualities mentioned in the first of this chapter. Our attitudes as well as our actions are always on trial before the youth of our churches. If we have a negative spirit, it permeates all that we do and all that we think. Youth tend to be like those whom they admire, and if they admire us and we are always negative, they will grow to be like that as well. On the other side of that coin is a positive attitude. Youth will just as soon pick up on a positive attitude as a negative one. Great care must be taken to keep our attitudes on a positive note.

Miscellaneous

I want to discuss just two more things before we go to some programming for modeling. One is speech. What we say and how we say it is important. The things about which we speak are very evident to youth, particularly, those who may constantly associate with us. Profane language and stories are completely out of the question for us if we are seeking to be all that God wants us to be, including being models for Christian discipleship. The other thing is related somewhat. The company we keep will influence us, and the places we go will give a good indication of the quality of our character. Great care must be taken.

Program

This section is not an attempt to enumerate all the programs of the Southern Baptist Convention that will be helpful to us as we seek to model our Christian lives for our youth. It will, however, serve as a springboard for further study if you are interested in some quality programming. A brief description follows each of the programs mentioned. More information can be found in your *Material Services Catalog* from the Baptist Sunday School Board.

DiscipleYouth

DiscipleYouth is a notebook of discipleship for youth. The concept is short term. The material begins with a booklet for a beginning retreat to encourage youth to be involved in discipleship on a continuing basis. One of the dynamics of this program is that the leader is a fellow learner. Modeling is a key to its success.

DiscipleLife Celebration

This is the ongoing youth discipleship program that is carried out in cooperation with the music ministry of the local church. It is guided by a published curriculum. The primary focus is that it is youth led. However, modeling or demonstrating on the part of the adult leader is an important function in the planning and implementing of this program. In addition to modeling, the adult leader needs to encourage the youth.

Continuing Witness Training

One of the important aspects of this program of evangelism in the church is the demonstration by the teacher of how to share one's faith with another person. A youth who may be interested in evangelism might really be encouraged to pursue this aspect of the Christian life if he or she saw a significant adult sharing his or her faith with another person.

DiscipleLife Centers

These are short-term studies for the development of discipleship principles in the lives of youth. An important aspect of these studies is the display of the principles taught by the adult who is teaching.

Equipping Centers

These, too, are short-term programs for the express purpose of showing people how to live the Christian life. Though they are not primarily designed for youth, the benefits for youth are very prominent.

Sunday School

The primary purpose of Youth Sunday School is not discipleship, but the teachers of youth in Sunday School as well as in other church programs must be willing to open their lives to the scrutiny of youth whom they teach. Youth must be able to see in their teachers that what they teach actually works.

Mission trips and Mission Projects

One of the most difficult areas of concern these days among youth is the concept of missions. Too many of us talk a good game about missions, but actually do little on a large scale. A great place for modeling the principles of the Christian life is a mission trip or project. Resource kits and other resources are available at your local Baptist Book Store to help you in this all important area.

Problems

Modeling the Christian life for those youth we are leading is difficult at best. It is very important, however. Frankly, discipleship is more caught than taught, so I want to point out two problems with the concept of modeling for the development of disciples.

The first one is the "Savior Complex." Youth leaders may have a tendency to think that just showing youth how to live as disciples will eliminate all difficulties. This is not true. We cannot save the whole world. God is in that business. We are to be God's agents, but our responsibility is not to save everyone. We must recognize our limitations. Realistically, we will probably only be able to develop a few relationships with youth who will see in us true discipleship. We must not be disappointed with that. We must do the best we can with what we have.

A second problem area is that of being real. A trap into which many folk fall is the trap of pretention. Great care must be taken by those of us who want to develop youth disciples to be real. Yes, we want to be positive models, but we do not want to fake our relationship with the Lord. Jesus showed us that He had difficulties with temptation and goals and human responses. He was always real and genuine in the expressions of His feelings to His disciples. What better model for us to do the same.

In conclusion, the world full of people crying for someone who will genuinely care about them. As adult leaders we have the opportunity of showing them that we not only care but that we are also developing youth who care. The bottom line for all of this is that we must commit ourselves to do discipling youth. It will not be easy, but it will be worth it.

Notes

1. John W. MacGorman, "Galatians," *The Broadman Bible Commentary*, Clifton J. Allen, gen. ed. (Nashville: Broadman Press, 1969-1971) 11:119.

2. Maxie D. Dunnam, *Galatians, Ephesians, Philippians, Colossians, Philemon, The Communicator's Commentary*, Lloyd J. Ogilvie, gen. ed. (Waco: Word Books, 1982) 8:116.

3. Ibid., p. 117.

4. William Barclay, *The Letters to the Galatians and Ephesians, The Daily Study Bible* (Edinburgh: The Saint Andrew Press, 1959), p. 56.

5. Olgilvie, p. 118.

6. MacGorman, p. 119.

7. Ibid.

8. Olgilvie, p. 119.

9. MacGorman, p. 120.

10. Clyde Hall and Joe Ford, *DiscipleYouth Kit* (Nashville: The Sunday School Board of the Southern Baptist Convention, 1982), pp. 22, 23.

11
Youth Discipleship
and Commitment Counseling
Art Criscoe

Introduction

Commitment counseling can be defined as a one-on-one relationship of interaction in which both the counselor and the youth seek guidance from the Bible. It is an integral part of youth discipleship. It is foundational. Youth must be guided and helped to get started in the right direction. Unless they receive effective counsel at key decision points in their lives, they may be hindered in their spiritual growth or even miss the way altogether.

This chapter examines the importance of commitment counseling with youth, the kind of person who makes a good counselor with youth, and three basic counseling skills. Guidelines are offered for three key commitments, and suggestions are given on where to go for additional help in learning counseling skills.

The Importance of Commitment Counseling with Youth

Youth live in that special period of life when key commitments are made related to discipleship. The youth years are formation years. Commitments made during this period, to a large degree, determine the shape, direction, and destiny of a person's life from that point forward.

Three young Hebrews named Hananiah, Mishael, and Azariah made commitments to God as teenagers. Years later they stood resolute with unflinching courage, refusing to give in to the decree of a pagan monarch to bow before an image. The Babylonian names of

Shadrach, Meshach, and Abednego rubbed off on them; the Chaldean culture did not. The commitments they made as youth served as a spiritual anchor and moral compass for the rest of their lives. Daniel, as an old man in his nineties, was guided by commitments he made as a youth. Joseph, David, Josiah, and Timothy are other biblical examples underscoring the life-changing effects of spiritual commitments made while youth.

To demonstrate the importance of youth making commitments to Christ, many evangelists often conduct impromptu surveys with congregations to determine the period of life when commitments were made to Christ. Invariably, the vast majority of Christians responding trusted Christ as Savior before reaching adulthood. If a youth graduates from high school as a non-Christian, researchers estimated that he or she has an 80 percent chance of going through life and dying unconverted.

Southern Baptist churches baptized 363,124 persons in 1986. Of this number, 54 percent or 195,955 were age 17 and under. In the age group 12 to 17, 86,387 people were baptized for 23.8 percent of the total number of baptisms.

Youth are free to choose. They are free to believe or not to believe. No one else can make a commitment for them. The decision is theirs individually. But a youth leader, parent, or other adult can offer wise counsel and encouragement to youth as they face key choices and decisions.

Youth have always needed support and counsel from adults as they faced turning points in life. This need is doubly true at present. Youth today are bombarded with a plethora of voices and pressures. The strongest influences on most youth are peers and media, both of which are not always in the best interest of the youth. The drug culture and other perverted subcultures offer youth a siren song. They grow up in a culture saturated with materialism and consumerism. Home and family life have eroded over the years. Youth often see a discrepancy between what adults say and how adults live.

The Person Who Counsels with Youth

What kind of person makes a good counselor with youth? What training is required to counsel effectively? Should commitment counseling with youth be restricted to the pastor and staff members? What about Joe and Sue, who work with a youth discipleship group on Sunday evening? Are they qualified to counsel? Fred teaches a group of older youth in Sunday School. Should he attempt to counsel with the youth in his class? Steve is a volunteer youth sponsor in the church. Would he make a good counselor? What about parents? Where do they fit in?

Professional training is not required for a person to be effective in counseling with youth. The important ministry of counseling youth should not be reserved for the pastor or other church staff members. Most likely, Joe, Sue, Fred, or Steve, as well as Mom and Dad, would make good counselors with youth.

What kind of person is effective in counseling with youth? What are the qualities or characteristics of a good youth counselor? At least four basic qualities or characteristics are found in effective counselors with youth.

A Growing Christian

A basic requirement for counseling with youth is a conversion experience. You can't lead someone somewhere you have not been yourself. A counselor should be a Christian and have assurance of salvation. A counselor's life should be characterized by spiritual growth—a dynamic, growing relationship with Christ.

A counselor should be an active member of his church. He should be firmly committed to the importance of the local church in God's redemptive plan. Bible study and prayer should be strong disciplines in the counselor's life.

A jingle expresses what youth intuitively know about adults who counsel with them.

Your talk talks
And your walk talks,

> But your walk talks
> More than your talk talks.

A counselor's "talk" is not worth very much unless it is backed up with a "walk." A counselor with youth is not necessarily a spiritual giant. It is essential, however, that the counselor be growing in his Christian life. Youth should know that the counselor has a growing relationship with Christ.

A Love and Concern for Youth

A youth counselor should possess a genuine interest in youth. She is motivated by Christian love and concern.

Early in Hebrew history God gave the command, "Thou shalt love thy neighbour as thyself" (Lev. 19:18 KJV). Jesus lifted this commandment to a place of high importance, second only to loving God (Matt. 22:37, 39). The key to loving youth is loving God with all our being. As we are committed to Him, we are able to reach out and love youth because He lives in us. We are able to express a measure of His love to the youth whom we counsel.

Love and concern for youth means that the counselor relates well with youth. She reaches out and builds rapport with them. She is easy to talk to, and youth are at ease and comfortable in her presence. This is important in youth counseling. Many times the young person is tense and does not communicate well. It is important for the youth to know that the counselor is really interested in him and wants to be of help.

Does Not Have All the Answers

That's right. The person who counsels with youth does not necessarily have all the correct answers and know all the right words to say. It is OK to say "I don't know." At times this is the only response the counselor can make.

This characteristic is actually an extension of the two preceding ones. Whereas the counselor's life is characterized by spiritual growth, she is not someone who has "arrived." She does not counsel youth from a position of superiority.

Paul wrote to the Roman Christians, "I beseech you therefore, brethren, by the mercies of God, that ye present your bodies a living sacrifice, holy, acceptable unto God, which is your reasonable service" (Rom. 12:1, KJV). The word "beseech" reveals Paul's attitude and approach. It is the Greek word *parakaleō* which is two words joined together, *beside* and *to call*. It means literally "to stand beside and call to." Paul was saying in this passage, "I stand beside you and appeal to you, I plead with you."

Paul's approach should characterize that of the person who counsels with youth. The counselor is a fellow traveler. The writer of Hebrews gave the admonition, "Let us run with patience the race that is set before us" (Heb. 12:1, KJV). The use of the pronoun "us" is revealing. At the time the letter was written, the writer identified himself with the recipients. He, too, was a runner in the race.

The youth counselor may be vulnerable. Strength can be found in weakness. Christ promised that His power would be strongest when we are weak (2 Cor. 12:9). There is an authenticity in relationships when the youth knows that the counselor, too, faces crisis points at times and also has questions as yet not fully answered.

Well-Adjusted

The youth counselor should possess a healthy outlook on life. He should be mentally and emotionally stable. He should not be hyper and easily excitable but steady and easygoing. He should not, either consciously or subconsciously, use the occasion of counseling youth as an opportunity to meet his own needs. Counseling youth is no place for aggressive and domineering behavior on the part of the counselor.

Counseling Skills

Whereas college or seminary training is not required for a person to counsel youth effectively, three basic commitment counseling skills are essential. These skills are not difficult to learn and can be developed by any adult who wishes to counsel youth. These skills are listening, communicating, and using Scripture.

Listening. Listening is basic in counseling youth. Because of her love and concern for youth, the counselor is interested in listening to them.

Empathy is important in listening. The counselor should try to put herself in the youth's place and understand what the youth is experiencing. Before the prophet Ezekiel counseled with the people, he identified with them and spent seven days with them. "I sat where they sat" (Ezek. 3:15, KJV). He looked at life through their window and wore their shoes.

Patience is an integral part of listening. The counselor does not rush ahead and do all of the talking. A steady flow of conversation is not necessary. Sometimes a period of silence is the right response. The counselor should be available and willing to listen as youth talk through feelings and emotions.

Eye contact is important in listening. Doodling on paper with a pencil, glancing at a wristwatch, or looking at the wall or out a window are signals to the youth that the counselor is not really listening to what he has to say.

Mental posture is basic in listening. The counselor should listen with objectivity. She observes the body language of the youth.

The counselor should recognize the barriers to effective listening. These barriers include not paying attention, distractions, excessive talking by the counselor, and personal biases. They all inhibit effective listening.

Communicating. Along with listening, communicating on a one-to-one basis is also primary in counseling youth. Here are five guidelines to help in communicating effectively.

- Create a climate of trust and confidence.
- Be positive and confident.
- Know what you want to say.
- Speak directly to the individual.
- Get feedback.

Among the many barriers that inhibit speaking are the same ones that inhibit listening. In addition, language itself can be a barrier. Words do not always have the same meaning to different persons. This is especially true of words used in commitment counseling like *faith, repent, believe, saved, heart, blood,* and *atonement.* The counselor must make sure that words and concepts are already understood.

Using Scripture. At the heart of commitment counseling with youth is communicating the good news. The Bible is God's Word. It does have the answers youth need. The counselor should possess a working knowledge of the Bible. He should know which Scripture passages speak directly to the specific needs, how to relate these passages to those needs of the youth, and how to explain these passages to the youth.

Counseling for Salvation. God does not have two plans of salvation. The Bible does not offer one way of salvation for adults and another for youth. There is only one way. A youth is saved just like an adult—by turning to Jesus Christ in repentance and faith.

However, youth may be at different developmental levels or may be struggling with some spiritual truth that most adults are already comfortable with. The counselor must be especially sensitive and clear when helping youth to make a commitment to Christ. The plan of salvation must be clearly explained in language they can understand. There is no place for manipulation or rushing through a decision.

If a youth has made a profession of faith as a child, that experience frequently is doubted and called into question during adolescence. Sometimes a child makes a decision and is baptized and received into the church without actually being converted. When doubts arise later as a youth, there is true conviction for the first time. The counselor is sensitive to recognize the youth's need and guides him to make a genuine commitment to Christ.

Other times a youth may doubt his earlier experience when in reality he did have an authentic experience of trusting Christ as Savior. A wise counselor listens patiently and offers caring affirmation of the validity of the youth's growing faith.

The Home Mission Board of the Southern Baptist Convention has developed a pamphlet, *Personal Commitment Guide,* for a counselor to use in commitment counseling. This *Personal Commitment Guide* gives step-by-step guidance for seven key commitments, the first one being salvation. A four-point outline for counseling relates to each type of commitment. These points are (1) God's purpose, (2) our need, (3) God's provision, and (4) our response. The counselor should carefully cover these four points when counseling a youth for salvation.

God's purpose for us can be summarized with the word *life.* He loves us and has a purpose for our lives—that we have eternal life. We receive eternal life as a free gift. We can live an abundant, full, and meaningful life right now, and we can spend eternity with Jesus in heaven. Helpful Scripture passages dealing with God's purpose include John 3:16; 10:10; 14:3; and Romans 6:23.

Our need also can be summarized with one word—*sin.* We are all sinners by nature and by choice. Sin is evil thoughts, words, and actions; it is missing the mark of God's standard. We deserve death and hell and cannot save ourselves. Some Scripture passages related to our need are Romans 3:23; 6:23; and Ephesians 2:9.

God's provision is a Person—*Jesus.* God is holy and just and must punish sin. Yet He loves us and provides a way for us to be forgiven. Jesus is God and became man. He died for us on the cross and arose from the dead. Scripture passages include John 1:1, 14; 14:6; 1 Peter 3:18; and Romans 4:25.

Our response involves repentance and faith. We must turn from our sin and turn to Jesus. We must surrender to Him or give Him control of our lives. Scripture passages include John 1:12; Acts 3:19; Ephesians 2:8; and Romans 10:9-10.

After explaining how to receive Christ, the counselor should help the youth to make her commitment to Christ. The youth should be guided to pray a prayer of commitment.

When a youth makes a commitment to Christ, the counselor should do both initial and extended follow-up. The subjects of assurance of salvation, baptism and church membership, and Christian growth should be discussed immediately. The *Survival Kit for New Christians,* Youth Edition, is an excellent resource to give the youth for extended follow-up. This eleven-week individualized course covers the basis of the Christian life and gets the youth started in a plan of quiet time, Bible study, Scripture memorization, prayer, and witnessing.

Counseling for Rededication. Rededication is the act of renewing one's commitment to Christ and reaffirming Christ's lordship. It is a time of confession of sin and yielding more completely to Christ. The Bible records many examples of rededication. Rededication is a common experience for many youth as they grow up physically and spiritually.

Reasons for youth rededicating their lives are as varied as youth themselves. Some specific sin may prompt the decision. There may have been a gradual drifting away from Christ. Changes in one's personal or family situation may prompt a rededication. An act of rededication can be an expression of a youth's desire to grow as a Christian. Special occasions, such as a birthday or the beginning of a new year, can prompt a youth to rededicate her life.

A counselor should help a youth take three actions in making a rededication. There should be: (1) confession of sin, (2) recommitment to the lordship of Christ, and (3) yielding daily to Christ. The counselor should encourage the youth to observe a quiet time each day. The four basic disciplines of Bible study, prayer, fellowship with other believers, and witnessing and ministering to others should be emphasized as means to Christian growth.

Counseling for Life's Vocation. Adolescence is a crucial period for youth in regard to their life's vocation. Affirming and caring counsel is needed to help them to serve and follow God's leading.

Our categories of *sacred* and *secular* are artificial and unbiblical. All of life is sacred. Churches usually stress God's call into full-time Christian vocational service and give a great deal of attention to youth who respond to this area. Other vocations and areas of life are often neglected.

The Bible clearly teaches that God calls every Christian to minister. The call to minister is a part of the call to salvation. The New Testament doctrine of the priesthood of believers affirms that God calls each Christian to witness and serve wherever he or she is. The work-place is not exempted. Each believer is to be a "marketplace mission-ary" in the circles and systems where he or she lives and works.

God has a plan for every life. God's perfect will includes a person's vocation. He leads His people into all areas of society and life. We have interpreted Jesus' command to go "into all the world" (Mark 16:15) in a geographical sense. However, we could also expand our concept of what it means to go into all the world to include vocation. When Jesus said that we are the salt of the earth and the light of the world, He clearly meant that Christians are to permeate all of society. We are to go into the world of teaching, the world of medicine, the world of law—everywhere—and influence that part of the world for Christ.

We sometimes fail to make this wider concept of calling clear to youth. They are searching for meaning and purpose and fulfillment. Sometimes they have never heard or understood that God's plan for their lives includes vocation. Some mistakenly think that the only way they can truly serve God is through a church vocation. Youth need to know that no area of work to which God leads is second class.

God does call some youth to church-related vocational service. These persons are called to an equipping ministry to help other believers fulfill their ministry.

Counselors need patiently to discuss and pray with youth regard-ing their life's vocation. They can help youth to identify their spiri-tual gifts. *We Have These Treasures: A Profile of Youth Leadership Gifts* by John Hendrix is a book that provides an instrument through which youth can discuss their leadership gifts. Counselors can help to in-troduce youth to the variety of expressions of ministry, both church related and nonchurch related.

Where to Go for Additional Help. Resources are available to equip all those who would do commitment counseling with youth. The *Personal Commitment Guide,* already referred to, is an indispensable aid that provides step-by-step guidance for most commitment counseling situations. *Commitment Counseling Manual* is a forty-eight-page booklet that trains a person in how to use the *Personal Commitment Guide.*

DecisionTime: Commitment Counseling is a comprehensive thirteen-session course that provides intensive training for counselors. It is a LIFE course provided by the Church Training Department.

Conclusion

Commitment counseling is a significant and fulfilling ministry as counselors lead youth in knowing and doing God's will. It is a ministry that should be Spirit led and undergirded with prayer.

12
Youth Discipleship and the Seasons of Life

Lela Hendrix

The Senior Club members had finished lunch and were gathered in the den for their last session of the year. The graduation ceremonies at their various schools were scheduled for that evening and through the weekend. The random chatter came to a focus when their sponsor threw out a question for discussion. She asked, "What is your dream? Tell us about the overarching dream, the umbrella goal, that will carry you through twenty years or more of your life."

With the question set before the older youth, the sponsor gave an example from her own life's journey: "A teacher in my high school said to me during the final days of my senior year, 'If you marry right away, you probably will never finish college. You are college material. You can do so much more with a college education. Don't stop with high school, please!' " The sponsor told the group that she made a vow to finish college. Her dream had been set in place, solidified by a challenge from a caring teacher. The sponsor said to her attentive audience, "Twenty years from the time the vow was made, when I finally graduated with a bachelor's degree, I said, 'Mrs. Roth, this one's for you.' "

The seniors listened to their sponsor's true-life story and then began to speak of their hopes and dreams. One eighteen-year-old young man started his sharing by saying, "The speaker at our church's senior-and-parent breakfast said that graduation means people will start asking, 'What are you doing to do?' The people who ask that question are wanting us to look down the pathway of life into thirty or forty years of our adult lives and say what will happen.

How can we answer the question when we are only teenagers? How can we see what life is like in the seasons of life yet to come? How do I know I will be able to even remember my high school days, my graduation, and my dreams?" Turning to his middle-aged sponsor, he asked, "Do you remember your graduation day? Will I be able to remember the events of this week when I'm forty-five?"

The questions of this older youth are an excellent example of the ones that face young Christian disciples. They ask: How do we know what lies ahead as we move through the stages of our adult lives? How do we know that we will know what to do when we get "there"? How do we know we can "keep the faith"? How do we know we will remember what life was like as a child or as a teenager? Who can tell us what it is like in the years yet to come? What are the seasons of life?

In the illustration from the Senior Club meeting, both the senior youth and the sponsor, representing two generations, spoke of situations in which they encountered learning about the upcoming seasons of life by interfacing with people who could provide information about the future. The sponsor spoke of a challenge created out of a relationship with an older woman, a teacher in her school. The senior youth spoke about an idea he had conceptualized while listening to an adult speak at the breakfast for seniors and their parents. He also felt free to ask questions of the Senior Club sponsor, an adult in middle adulthood. These two people, the senior and the sponsor, had persons in their lives who could assist them in looking ahead. In the context of providing discipleship training to youth in our churches, we can provide relationships. We can surround youth with persons who can help them ask the right questions and seek the right answers about what lies ahead in life. As adults, we play a vital role, but we must ask ourselves if we feel any sense of urgency, an urgency about doing what we do best, that is, live our lives and share from our life story.

Equipping Youth with a Sense of Urgency

Discipling youth requires a sense of urgency. This sense of urgency is necessary because youth will not stay youth. They will all too quickly become adults too. This sense of urgency comes from a desire to lead youth to Christ and equip them to be disciples at the earliest possible stage of life—in the morning of their days, in the spring of their seasons. If adult leaders believe that all times are in God's hands, they believe that there is not a day, a year, or a season of life in which God is not present. God is shaping, turning, molding the direction of our lives. Like the potter at the wheel, like the captain at the controls, like the designer of special creations, God is at work. In the family of God, all children, all youth, and all adults find purpose and meaning because God endows each life with the ability to find meaning.

To guide youth to a life that journeys toward foreverness with God, we as leaders must see the value in presenting the challenge of a discipled life to children and youth who are a part of our journey. Many adult leaders know that to walk with God in the early morning hours of life is to enjoy the walk with God in the twilight years of life. Our experience has taught us that to plant the seed of a fruitful life in the spring of our existence is to reap the fruit of fall and move into the winter season with the assurance that God's presence is with us.

As adult leaders who recognize the urgency in being responsible to the task of discipling youth, we also recognize that we want to be true to our own search for meaning at each season of life. Our words and deeds are to be those of men and women who are experiencing God in each stage of adulthood. Youth are quick to catch the subtle nuances in what we say. They are quick to point out the inconsistencies in our words and actions. They are quick to distinguish the hidden meanings. In their borderline existence between child and adult, they bounce between being an adapted child who is doing as we do and saying what we say because they want to be like us and being the natural child who does what comes naturally because of their natural childlikeness. Youth are watching adult role models and listening to adult speakers with a certain criticalness. As adult leaders we must constantly be aware of our journey and the meaning we find in the living of our days. Out of the adult's sense of urgency about the search for meaning and the adult's willingness to share the struggle, youth discover the process for their journeying.

Our endeavors as leaders of youth will take on urgency if we visualize youth as needing what God has to offer: salvation and discipleship. What urgency do you feel about equipping youth to find God's will and direction for the journey of a lifetime?

Equipping Youth for a Lifelong Pilmgrimage

The psalmist said with assurance, "How blessed is the man whose strength is in Thee; In whose heart are the highways to Zion!" (Ps. 84:5-6, NASB).

How blessed are the youth whose hearts are focused on a direction that leads into God's kingdom. How blessed are the ones who will turn the deserts and valleys of life into growing experiences that lead to bubbling springs and lofty mountaintops.

Adults can equip youth to see the peaks and valleys of the journey in such a way that they can face tomorrow with dreams and assurance, knowing that the pathway is not always smooth and straight. In discipling youth, we can present realism that helps them shape their idealism. The task includes assisting them to see balance between what can be and what might be. The task is to present the Christian life as a series of ongoing meaningful events rather than a one-time decision, reminding them that quality and quantity are more than the sum of their times and seasons. The task is to stretch the growing capabilities of youth by presenting challenges that pull them toward the future. The task is to help youth discover their uniqueness in God's creation by reminding them that the concept of eternity placed in their mind and life's journey, with its element of foreverness, is filled with times and seasons.

Equipping Youth to Discover the Seasons of Life

The term *life cycle* has two implications about how life develops. One picture is the process of journey from birth to death. The movement through the years follows a basic pattern with sequential tasks and achievements through which all people move. The other picture of the life cycle is not a simple, continuous, unchanging flowing, rather it is like seasons. In each season distinctive elements occur. In each season certain tasks must be accomplished relatively well before the person can move successfully into the next season.

The seasons of life with their varied tasks have been categorized differently by theorists, with age ranges suggested by some. Age ranges, although easy to use, are blurry and fuzzy. Age is not a good predictor of timing. Seasons, then, suggests sequence but not specific intervals: spring with the childhood and youth tasks, summer with the young adult tasks, fall with the middle adulthood tasks, and winter with the tasks of senior adults. Each season has its tasks, a right time in which certain things are to be accomplished. This is more obvious during the childhood and youth years, but the principle remains the same throughout the adult years of life.

In *All Times Are God's Seasons* the tasks of adolescence, early, middle, and later adulthood are presented.[1] These tasks are based on the developmental skills that have started in childhood and continue into youth and adult seasons of life.

Tasks of Adolescence

1. Achieving better relations with age-mates of both sexes
2. Accepting the masculine or feminine social role
3. Accepting one's body and using one's body with personal satisfaction
4. Becoming free from childish dependence on parents; developing affection for parents without dependence upon them
5. Developing a positive attitude toward family life
6. Beginning plans for achieving a career and making a living

7. Deciding what is important as a guide for behavior
8. Participating as a responsible person in the life of the community

Tasks of Early Adulthood

1. Making choices about marriage
2. Selecting a mate
3. If one marries . . .
   - Learning to live with a marriage partner
   - Successfully starting a family
   - Meeting the physical and emotional needs of children
4. Managing a home
5. Getting started in an occupation
6. Taking on civic responsibility

Tasks of Middle Age

1. Assisting teenage children to become responsible, happy adults
2. Assuming adult social and civic responsibility
3. Reaching and maintaining satisfactory performance in a career
4. Developing adult leisuretime activities
5. Continuing to relate to one's spouse in a significant way
6. Accepting and adjusting to the changes of middle age
7. Adjusting to aging parents

Tasks of Later Adulthood

1. Adjusting to decreasing physical strength and health
2. Adjusting to retirement and reduced income
3. Adjusting to the death of a spouse
4. Accepting one's place as a member of the elders of society
5. Adopting and adapting new and flexible social roles
6. Establishing satisfactory physical living arrangements

   Life, when viewed as seasons, is a lifelong process of change. Learning can occur every moment, and the term *lifelong learning* takes on exciting meaning. Youth and young adulthood do not signal the end of education when all of life is seen as a time for learning. All along the journey are places, like plateaus, where the learner pauses to catch a breath before moving rapidly along once more. Interspersed in the rough times—the transitions—are periods of calm and stability. Equipping youth to identify the tasks in life is essential in youth discipleship training. Discipleship is a lifelong learning process, full of growth and change, and youth will discover new opportunities for utilizing their God giftedness in each season.

Equipping Youth to Tell Time

Leaders and parents of small children go to great measures to teach the little ones how to tell time. Youth require help in telling time too. Youth need assistance in distinguishing between kinds of time. How do we teach time to the teenager?

The Bible distinguishes between two kinds of time—*chronos* time and *kairos* time. *Chronos* time is time in intervals and sequence—quantity time. We get our word *chronology* from this word. We ask, "What is your age?" and expect an answer in years, months, and days. We ask, "What time?" and expect an hour and minute response. Early in life, most people learn to tell *chronos* time.

The other time is *kairos* time—quality time, time with meaning, time tied to a particular stage or season of life, time related to specific events. We ask, "What happened in your adolescence?" and expect an answer about problems, joys, feelings, and events during that stage of life. The questions about quality time are not answered with hour, week, and year responses. Many people never learn to tell *kairos* time.

Equipping youth to distinguish between *chronos* time and *kairos* time involves helping them to identify "foreverness." As persons move from the childhood of life into the youth stage of life, the capacity for abstract thinking begins to develop. Youth can utilize both the abstract and concrete modes of thinking. With the onset of this capability, the terms *foreverness* and *eternity* can be conceptualized.

The significance of this new way of seeing life is that one's physical existence on Earth takes on a different meaning. The living of the "days of one's life" is placed in the context of a continued existence in God's family.

The task of equipping youth to discover that life has the added dimension of foreverness includes helping them stretch their mental, moral, and spiritual capacities. In recent decades, the term *quality of life* has taken on popularity related to social issues; however, the Bible has been the resource for this way of evaluating life long before the social science experts picked it up to distinguish between the length of one's days and the meaning of one's life. For the Christian, the quality of life is shaped and molded by one's response to God. In the years of adolescence, the ability to make wise choices has impact upon the quality of life as well as the quantity of life. The task of equipping youth is to stretch their mental and spiritual capacities in order that their choices during these early developmental stages will be maximized.

Equipping Youth to Live Relationally in God's Family

In recent decades, youth have been introduced into the work force during their middle teen years. Economically, the lines separating the ages of the work force are blurring. Socially, the average age when men and women marry is in the early twenties; however, the age for having children is causing concern—children are having children, and middle age women are choosing to have first children at later ages—late thirties and early forties. The age for having children may be limited in *chronos* years, yet parenting is being done by children and adults, even senior adults, in *kairos* time. These examples are indications that blurring is occuring in age-defined stages of life.

Although the blurring of age appears to be making the lines between youth and adulthood less obvious in *chronos* time, the youth stage of life in American society still has a place in *kairos* time. The spring season of life—the adolescent stage with its tasks—is essential in the sequence. To pass from childhood to adulthood, to eliminate the spring season, is to bring a prematureness to life that can be hazardous. The eliminating of seasons or stages of life is to rob life of its naturalness and intention. In God's family, all people and all times are important and meaningful.

As youth, the season of spring is a time of rapid growth and change. Many times the rapidity of the development leaves the youth unable to look ahead with any certainty that the future is worth the living. Relationships are in jeopardy with many people due to circumstances beyond the control of teenagers and children. The socialization toward separation from relational living seems greater for young men than for the young women in current American life; and for youth as a whole, there is a trend to separate them as an age group. When youth become separated from their sources of care giving too early, either individually or as a group in a specific culture, the feelings of independence and segregation can lead them away from close relationships.

In the family of God, in the church congregation, and in the family unit, youth are to be included, not excluded. Youth are not to be segregated from the congregated. Youth are significant and necessary to the life of those younger and those older. Youth are a part of the journey.

Equipping Youth with Specific Techniques

To equip youth to recognize the seasons of life and to welcome the opportunities inherent in each season, certain teaching techniques and activities can be selected to strengthen their learning.

Some of the teaching techniques suggested are the common, everyday garden variety that are utilized with youth in effective discipleship training sessions; however, suggesting the design of specific programs for youth with an emphasis on interaction with persons from seasons of life different than their own will be a new concept in many youth programs. *Intentionally* is the key word. Discipleship training that focuses on the seasons of life must include using intergenerational learning settings and teaching techniques that create a sharing of life's journey as well as a sharing of life's stories with people of all ages.

To enhance discipleship training, review the techniques and suggestions provided. Then be creative in adapting these general ideas to the specific topics being selected for youth discipleship sessions.

Inductive Approaches to Bible Study

Facts and basic concepts about what Christians believe are essential to inductive Bible study. Certainly youth leaders will want to be sure the foundation is firm. In the youth years, the use of the facts can be accentuated by pulling forth from the youth the application, the insights, and the possibilities of the faith facts.

Presentation of Christian Values

Youth years are the beginning of the seasons of life for expanding from a strict belief in the literal facts about life to the choosing of certain, specific facts about life. The development of a personal value system begins in adolescence and, hopefully, continues on through adulthood. One counselor, when asked why a young man kept making such bad choices for his life, said about the situation, "How can the youth make decisions between good and bad if all he has learned is bad." In a world that presents the opposite view of Christian values, adult leaders in discipleship groups have an opportunity to present values with the Christian emphasis.

Practice in Decision Making

For the adults to present only facts and express their own prized values is not enough. Youth need opportunities to make decisions for themselves. Practice sessions are helpful. Sharing leadership and calling forth the strengths of youth, allowing them to be doers not just hearers, are two avenues for letting them make decisions under the tutorage of caring adults.

Involvement in Simulated Experiences

To involve youth in simulated or nearly "real" learning activities that ask them to make choices about what they want from life's cafeteria of experiences is getting them to think ahead for the upcoming realities of life. So many of life's experiences carry drastic, irreversible consequences. We should try to protect youth from having to learn some truths from firsthand knowledge. Teaching about the next season with its many decisions can be done in "playlike" sessions. The learning may not be as quick, but wisdom is to learn from the experience of others. Youth can be wise.

Encouragement in Spiritual Disciplines

Youth can be very, very spiritual. The emotions are active, the senses are becoming finely tuned, the ability to be reflective is operative, the existential search for meaning is intensified as a youth approaches the end of the teen years—all the criteria for finding and making contact with God are present. Youth are amazing. They can often hide their spiritual nature from adults. When confronted, they will admit that they long to be spiritually attuned. At this season, the search for the one to whom they make their attachment is crucial. Youth who make their attachment to God firm and fixed in the spring season of life can build upon that early choice as they strive to bring quality to the quantity of life.

Programming for Personal Growth

Youth need never grow old. Have you as an adult been asked, "Do you remember what it was like to be a teenager?" Can you remember? Probably you can. Youth need reassurance that they will remember. Youth need never grow old; however, youth need to advance through the spring season and move on. To hold on to adolescent qualities can be negative when one is expected to behave like an adult. Programs and activities that encourage youth to grow and change call the youth to move on into the next season of life. Guidance and encouragement from growing adults not only gives verbal challenge but provides role modeling of how painful and joyful growth can be.

Intentional Involvement of Youth with People of All Ages

With the tendencies for youth to be separated and segregated from other age groups, the intentional involvement of youth has become a necessity in youth ministry, not a luxury. The involvement can be in a variety of ways including service projects, study groups, parent/leader/youth fellowships, retreats, and utilization of youth in leadership roles with younger children. The placement of youth with people of other ages will not guarantee that youth will mix or relate. The structuring of the time together must be designed to facilitate the interaction.

Intergenerational Activities and Studies

The use of intergenerational settings for teaching youth is not common to many congregations. Although the need to learn how to work with people of all ages in one group is being felt among some leaders, the need is still low priority. The resources for intergenerational programming are limited. Some time in future years, the time will be right for stronger intergenerational emphases. To learn about the seasons of life, youth can observe children and see what has happened to them in previous stages of development. Youth can look at the stage adjacent to theirs, the young adult, and readily observe what is coming up next. Youth can observe the middle and older adults and learn from their mistakes and successes. In the context of church programming, attention must be given to structuring new groups for learning.

Storytelling with People of All Ages

Nothing is as captivating as a story. Everyone has a story and a story to tell. The Christian faith is built on story—God's story, told and retold through the ages. The seasons of life are always present in real life stories. The institutional form of teaching in the Judeo-Christian religion must surely be the story technique. The personal story is sometimes the best one. The simple, the most profound. Leaders of youth have a story. Youth have a story. Let us each tell our story—from generation to generation, from season to season.

Note

1. *All Times Are God's Seasons* John & Lela Hendrix (Nashville: Convention Press, 1986), pp. 34, 41, 53, 66.

13
Youth Discipleship
and Peer Pressure/Ministry
Lamar Slay

Dawson McAllister, who speaks to thousands of teenagers every year, gives the following definition of peer pressure, "Peer pressure is the pressure we receive from those around us to follow or accept their standards of conduct, way of thinking, and values in life." There is probably no greater force involved in our youth's lives than that of peer pressure. Peer pressure has always affected the way our students live and respond to the gospel of Jesus Christ. It becomes an increasingly important issue when Christian teenagers are asked to take their stand on their campus.

The purpose of this chapter is to deal with the issue of peer pressure from two perspectives. First, we will look at the aspect of training our teenagers to overcome peer pressure on their campus through discipleship. The second part of this chapter will deal with getting the students involved in a peer group ministry. The only way that peer group ministry can take place in our youth groups is if those who are involved in the ministry have a solid handle personally in dealing with peer pressure. Most students today find it difficult to take a stand on campus, much less to aggressively speak out and be a leader in ministering to other students.

Peer Pressure

Ten principles need to be taught to our youth to help them overcome peer pressure. The needs of every youth group are different. The topics of these principles need to be taught through a discipling ministry tailored to the specific youth group. The resources that can be used are almost unlimited and may be found in many Christian book stores. Depending on the youth group, one particular principle may need to be dealt with more extensively than others.

Principle #1: Youth must be taught to
develop a strong personal walk with God.

The key to overcoming the effects of peer pressure in any young person's life is his personal walk with God. Regardless of the number of courses we teach our young people, or the number of retreats or camps we take them on, the bottom line is that their personal walk with God must be strong, aggressive, and growing. Daniel 3, records the story of three young Hebrew boys who overcame tremendous peer pressure to take their stand for God. It is a classic example to use in teaching teenagers how they, too, can overcome that pressure in their lives. Shadrach, Meshach, and Abed-nego had every reason to bow down to the statute that King Nebuchadnezzar had made. But in the face of tremendous odds, they took their stand and defied the pressure that was thrust upon them.

God honored the youth's stand, and in the end they won the victory. As the three youth stood together, they were eventually exalted, and an entire nation was lead to bow down to their God. This very same thing can happen on campuses throughout our country today if youth ministers will be diligent to train and equip their students to take a stand on campus. The key to overcoming peer pressure on the part of students is not what they know, but who they know. One of the greatest things that we can teach teenagers today is how to spend time with God on a daily basis. Many techniques and materials are available to aid in that learning process. Teenagers should be encouraged to have a daily quiet time and then taught how to do so by their spiritual leaders.

Principle #2: Young people must be led to understand who they
are in Christ both spiritually and physically.

Oftentimes we fail to teach young people what they have in Jesus Christ. We are told in 2 Corinthians 5:17 that when we come to

Christ, we are made brand new. We are told that the old things pass away, and, "behold, all things are become new" (KJV). One of the greatest needs that young people have today is the need to be accepted by their peers. This often leads them to do things that go against their own personal convictions. If we can teach them that in Christ they are totally complete and do not need the acceptance of their friends to be complete, we have taken a giant step in helping them to overcome peer pressure.

Young people need to be shown not only that they are totally complete in Christ but also that they have absolutely everything that they need to be successful in life. The world says that in order to be successful on their campus, they need to be accepted by the "right" group of people, to have the "right" friends, and to be invited to the "right" social events. God's Word tells us that in Christ they are totally complete and totally accepted by Him. We can take a lot of pressure off the kids to succeed in the things of the world by showing them that God's Word says their success rests in Jesus Christ and not in their peer group.

The second area young people need to understand is the area of their physical appearance. Volumes have been written about the struggle adolescents go through as they enter the teenage years and begin to "find themselves." As we teach them that they are acceptable to God the way they are, we can help them put less emphasis on the things of the world such as clothing and appearance and more emphasis on spiritual things. Young people need to see that they do not need the acceptance and praise of their peer group in order to be complete but that in Christ Jesus they are complete. Jeremiah 1:5 tells us that God was involved in creating us before we were even born. Young people were not afterthoughts but divine creations of the almighty God to fulfill the purpose that He has for them in their lives.

Principle #3: Young people need to be taught a strong intimate relationship with their parents.

The young person's relationship with her parents is the most important relationship that she will ever experience. If that relationship at home is not healthy, the teenager will seek to develop alternative relationships outside of the home. This often leads to the teenager getting involved with a crowd or a group of people that does not necessarily share her spiritual or moral values.

A young person is going to seek acceptance. God's design is for that acceptance to come from the teen's parents. If that does not take place, she will find that acceptance outside of the home. It is vital that we teach our young people that great importance should be put on their relationship with their parents. In our ministries, we need to reinforce the role of the parents in young people's lives as well as aid those parents in being creative in building that relationship. Our teenagers need to be accepted at home, so they are not constantly seeking it elsewhere.

Principle #4: Young people must be taught to develop a standard of moral behavior that is based on Scripture and not on the world's standards.

Most teenagers develop standards for moral behavior based on four things: (1) friends; (2) the media—music, movies, TV; (3) their parents; (4) personal convictions. Young people must be taught to develop their standard of behavior based on God's Word alone. Most of our young people know more lyrics to popular songs than they do Scripture.

As we teach young people to turn to God's Word for answers, we must show them the fallacy of the philosophies put forth in the latest songs they hear on the radio, movies they see in the theater, and programs they watch on TV. The media has a profound effect on the values and behaviors of even our finest church young people.

We must show them how relevant God's Word is in their lives today. Second Timothy 3:16 teaches us that God's Word is good not only for "teaching" but also for "reproof, for correction, and for training." This must become the guidelines by which our young people judge their activities. We cannot become the one in their life to tell them if a particular event or activity is right or wrong; rather, we must lead them to rely on the power of the Holy Spirit as He speaks to them through God's Word.

Principle #5: Young people must be taught to choose their friends carefully.

First Corinthians 15:33 teaches us that "bad company corrupts good morals" (NASB), and this is not seen any clearer than in the lives of teenagers today. But we must do more than teach teenagers not to choose bad friends; we must also challenge them to actively seek friends who will inspire them to live for God. They need a Christian peer group.

While it is important for Christian teenagers to have acquaintances who are lost for the sake of evangelism, we must teach them to surround themselves with their closest friends who have like spiritual convictions and life-styles. One of the greatest areas of conflict that teenagers have with their parents is over the matter of friends. If we can help them establish criteria by which they choose their friends, we can aid them tremendously in their homes.

Principle #6: Young people must be taught to determine their activities based on their moral values and good judgment.

Youth ministers must teach young people what is evil in the sight of God and must lead them to hold strong moral convictions based on their own study of God's Word. While adult leaders find soapbox lecturing easy when the topics include condemning party going, casual sex, strong emphasis on possessions and status, and other things that are scripturally wrong, leading teenagers to make those convictions their own is harder. We must disciple them in walking daily with the Father. This responsibility becomes even greater when we realize that, for the most part, the media is reinforcing their minds with the exact opposite of what God's Word teaches.

**Principle #7: Young people must be taught to
emphasize the eternal and not the temporal.**

Teenagers today live in a society that on every hand emphasizes living for the moment and not worrying about the future. Society can also give the impression that the future is pretty bleak. Many illustrations can be given from today's newspapers concerning athletes and other popular personalities who lived for the moment and threw away their future. As young people are taught that Christians should place emphasis on things that are permanent, as in the spiritual realm, the things of the present can become less and less important to them. The church must help them put the emphasis in the areas of their lives that will make a difference in how they live for God in the future.

**Principle #8: Young people must be led to make the
decision to be a positive force on their campus
as they seek to influence it for Christ.**

Teaching our young people to live by the power of the Holy Spirit is not enough. If we are to reach our world for Christ and see vast numbers of teenagers come to know Him, we must teach our youth to be aggressive in sharing their faith on campus. They must be taught to share their faith verbally and through the example of their life-styles and moral behavior. The first step to their witness is for them to live a godly life before their peers. Only as they have a life that backs up their conversation will they have credibility with other students on their campus.

**Principle #9: Young people must be taught to live under the
lordship of Jesus by the power of the Holy Spirit.**

Romans 12:1-2 admonishes us to present ourselves as sacrifices to the Father. Acts 1:8 tells us that we will have the power to be the witnesses that God intends for us to be. Regardless of the number of seminars or discipleship groups we put our young people through, if we do not teach them the secret of relying on the power of the Holy

Spirit and of making Jesus their Lord, we have failed them. Young people may forget the greatest discipleship lesson they were ever taught or the greatest sermon they ever heard. But if we can teach them how to walk with Jesus on a daily basis and rely on the power on the Holy Spirit, they will never be the same.

Principle #10: Young people must be committed to the James 1:22 principle.

James 1:22 states, "Prove yourself doers of the word and not merely hearers who delude themselves" (NASB). True discipleship results in changed behavior. Many young people today know more than they are living on a day-to-day basis. Many of them know more than they are telling when it comes to sharing their faith. Our responsibility as their spiritual leaders is to challenge and motivate them to put into action what they learn in the small groups. As spiritual principles are learned, they must be lived or they are useless in our lives. Unless our young people put into practice what they are taught, we as their teachers have failed. We need young people to be doers and not just hearers.

Peer Group Ministry

After we have discipled in the area of overcoming peer pressure, we need to involve youth in ministering to their peers. Throughout the New Testament, Jesus is shown involving the disciples in ministry. He saw His ministry through the eyes of the twelve men He had chosen. Regardless of how effective local youth ministers are in their churches and on the campuses in their towns, they will never be able to have the impact on students that other students can have.

In order for a ministry to students to be effective, it must involve students ministering to other students. At Castle Hills First Baptist Church in San Antonio, Texas, we developed a ministry to students that was based on the students themselves actually doing the work of the ministry. It involved a group of students known as "Team Leaders" who were responsible for inreach through the Sunday School organization. The result of the team leader ministry was tremendous growth in Sunday School, as well as the other youth organizations. While the plan of the ministry itself is very simple, some basic principles must be followed in order for a peer group ministry to be successful.

Recruitment of Team Leaders

Team leaders were recruited during the two months prior to church program organization promotion. We attempted to recruit team leaders in every department in Youth Sunday School, beginning with the seventh grade and going through the twelvth grade. While general announcements and written ads were made for team leaders, the Sunday School teachers and youth staff members actively recruited specific individuals whom we felt would be effective in this type of ministry. From the beginning, we were more concerned with the quality of the team leaders than we were with quantity. We knew that in some areas we would not have enough team leaders to cover the Sunday School enrollment, but we could fall back on the volunteer adult youth workers to minister to those students. Any young person who was willing to make the commitment, attend the training, and minister to a group of students was allowed to sign up to be a team leader. Each year we were surprised by some of the students who came forward and became very effective team leaders.

Midway through the church year, we usually had a second team leader recruitment time. This allowed us to increase the number of team leaders we had to help minister to the new students we were reaching, as well as add additional team leaders to any department in which we were understaffed. While the second group of recruits was usually small, we always picked up some quality team leaders to be involved in the ministry.

Training Team Leaders

The training of the team leaders took two forms. The initial training usually involved either a retreat away from the church or a weekend of training at the church. This occurred at the beginning of the year and at the halfway point after the second phase of recruitment. Ongoing training occurred once a month at our regular team leader training meeting.

The training involved basic ministry skills and principles. We taught the team leaders how to look beyond the surface problems of their peers and to see the real spiritual needs. We dealt with the basics of carrying on a conversation and turning that conversation to a spiritual conversation. We did much training in the area of personal evangelism by helping the students learn how to effectively find the spiritual condition of the students for whom they were responsible. We encouraged our students to get involved in some form of evangelism training that was offered at our church. We also did some specialized training in the area of helping teenagers deal with broken homes and other crises they would face in dealing with their peers.

Commitment Involved in Being a Team Leader

In the recruitment stage, we stated that team leaders were expected to be youth who had a strong personal walk with God. This involved their having a daily quiet time and a willingness to be involved in Scripture memorization. It also involved their being active in all of the major programs of the youth ministry, particularly in the Bible study program on Sunday morning.

Team leaders were asked to take the responsibility of staying in touch and ministering to approximately eight to twelve of their peers. This involved a minimum of one contact per month concerning the spiritual needs of each person. They were also asked to attend a meeting once a month where they would give a written report of the contacts they had made with their group of students during the previous month. We found very quickly that accountability was a key ingredient to the success of a team leader program.

Composition of Team Leader's Groups

The team leader's groups were divided by sex and department. In other words, a ninth grade boy team leader would only have ninth grade boys in his group. We also attempted to divide the groups geographically, as far as possible, so that a student's group members would possibly attend the same school. In a metropolitan situation, this was obviously very difficult to do, although it tremendously aided in ministry. However, the majority of contacts made by team leaders would be made by telephone. We also attempted to put a mixture of active and inactive youth in each group.

No more than twelve students were put in a team leader's group. This principle was adhered to even if it meant that some of our students were not assigned to a group at the beginning of the year. Twelve simply is the maximum number of students another student can effectively keep up with during the course of a month.

Team Leaders Relating to Adults

A key ingredient to the team leader program was the way the team leaders and their groups related to the adult youth workers in their Sunday School department. Each youth Sunday School teacher was assigned two team leaders and their groups as their class roll. This gave the teacher two group leaders to help him minister to the students for whom he was responsible. The team leaders would share not only their reports at the monthly team leader meetings but also on a week-to-week basis with their Sunday School teachers. If there were a specific need the teacher should be made aware of in a student's life, this report would highlight that. This team effort was very productive and fruitful in reaching not only the regular youth but perimeter students as well.

Materials for Team Leaders

The materials for carrying out the team leader program were very simple but very important. Each team leader was given a list of the young people on his or her team that included phone numbers and addresses. These lists were put into an inexpensive notebook and given to the team leaders. They were asked to bring these notebooks with them on Sundays as well as to the once-a-month team leader meeting. All training notes and other materials that were handed out to them were then put in the notebook where they could be kept up with easily. It became a very positive thing for our team leaders to be seen with their notebooks, thus denoting that they had a position of leadership within the youth ministry. Tabs were put into the notebook for them to keep their prayer lists and daily devotional journals. Therefore, our team leaders needed only one notebook.

Conclusion

The team leader program is nothing more than a revamping of the "group leader" concept used by Adult Sunday School departments. While it is not *the* answer, it is a key ingredient in ministering to youth. When we do the ministry for our youth, it is our ministry. When we involve them, it becomes their ministry. Expand your ministry with youth by letting it become their ministry.

14
Youth Discipleship and the Influence of Media
Randy Lanford

Media has a significant influence on our youth. It has an impact that goes beyond the easy-to-observe and record number of hours of television they watch, amount of money spent on the latest cassette tapes, or the popularity of the current teen exploitation film. It can be that subversive, silent, almost insidious influence that gradually changes our youth into creatures distant from the creation God intended.

Media, in this chapter, refer to means of communication. Media are methods for conveying a subject or idea to a person or group of persons. The three primary media are print, audio, and visual. I will focus primarily on the latter two and the influence they have on youth today.

Every medium has its good and bad points. History has shown us that the invention and development of any new technology or product issues in changes that affect our lives. What may appear to be a simple, time saving improvement in our lives may later show negative side effects. Television can be a unifier of our entire nation as it scatters the same information from coast to coast at the same time. A majority of people will hear the information if it is put on the airwaves at the right time for the audience desired. Television could bring people the finest in theater, art, music, literature, and so forth, although it has not done so consistently yet.

The printing press is an example of an obvious improvement that is not without negative side effects. When first developed it exhibited some of this immediate good and later bad dichotomy. Very few people would argue against the great importance of the printing press. It obviously moved communication into a new era. But it also downgraded oral tradition. We have experienced loss in the art of storytelling. Verbal communication has diminished, and the great need for the wisdom of the aged has been replaced by the printed word. What need do we have for people who lived through an event of historical significance when we can quickly turn to a book on the subject written by a self-proclaimed expert in the field?

God is a giver of good gifts. He desires the best for His children. God can even be seen as the source of the wisdom man has used to produce many of the electronic/mechanical media that influence our lives. God has given us many advantages in the cultures we live in. But as with so many things in this life, hindrances abound within the advantages of our culture. We must be aware of the disadvantages as well as the advantages of our culture. Media are *not* neutral. They affect us beyond the absolutely ambiguous visual/auditory medium. Media, in all its forms, are teaching systems. Our youth are learning from them at an alarming rate. What they are learning is not always as apparent as the picture they are viewing or the music they are hearing.

Those of us involved in discipleship are faced with teaching systems that have our youth much more than we do. Television/movies/radio have them almost a majority of their day.

We are forced into the position of educating children who have been conditioned to respond to learning settings in a certain way. We should not be surprised when young persons are involved otherwise or sleeping during our weightiest worship or Bible study. They have experienced years of being able to half listen or totally disregard the authority person or situation on the television and not suffer any reproach or correction. They may not be premeditatively rude. They are responding as they do to television all day long. If the program is boring, they turn the channel. If the weather or news comes on the radio, they change stations. If the movie is not funny, they sneak into the theater next door. And in all of these situations, seldom is a real, live, breathing, caring human being available to help them decide which is the more important activity.

Everybody seems to know that television is exerting a profound influence on our youth although we are not always clear as to what it is. Contrast the amount of time in school, watching television (tapes), listening to the radio, attending movies, and time at home with the amount of time spent in church each week. The simplest breakdown of these figures will show that youth spend about 1 percent of their time at church, 16 percent of their time at school and 83 percent of their time at home (much of that is asleep). What are the different compulsions that bring youth to: School? The law/legal compulsion. Television? A psychological compulsion. Church/discipleship? A spiritual compulsion. Television is centered on attention; school, on content; church, on both. In school if a student does not pay attention, she is removed from the class. In television if a youth does not pay attention, the "teacher" is removed from the airwaves "class." In the world where youth are in the presence of media, if the sitcom, movie, or music is not a "good teacher" (defined as an entertainer who holds their attention), they influence ratings by not watching, not attending, or not buying. Soon the "teacher" is changed as producers, sponsors, and investers move their money to a medium which will involve more viewers, listeners, or purchasers.

Television consists of picture stories. Discipleship is mainly a word-centered exposition. On television the picture is most important. It is principally a visual medium. We *watch* television. Between the ages of five and eighteen a youngster will see approximately 675,000 commercials, at the rate of about 1,000 per week. This makes the television commercial the most voluminous information source in the education of youth. Our youth are being conditioned to intense concentration for short periods of time and "deconditioned" to sustained concentration. This will have an effect on the methods we use to present discipleship to youth.

Youth respond to long lectures by turning us off. Anything over eight to ten minutes without a substantial change of focus or dynamic difference is lost on them. Television has conditioned them to expect frequent changes and has made it difficult for them to sustain a fixed point of view. Researchers point to decreased linguistic and writing skills as being partially due to the television-centered existence of our children and youth.

Discipleship is learning within the context of a relationship. To try to imagine a person discipled without handson, face-to-face time with another believer is incongruous. Discipleship by way of the cassette tape or video player may be a reality, but I feel it is less than an accurate transmission of our Lord's desires for discipleship. Jesus came to earth in the form of man when the medium of spoken word, written word, and visual illustration failed to communicate the message of God adequately. Your personal, intimate, face-to-face relationship with youth is more important to your accomplishment of this definition of discipleship:

> *Discipleship* is the Christian's lifelong commitment to the person, teaching, and spirit of Jesus Christ. Life under Jesus' Lordship involves progressive learning, growth in Christlikeness, application of biblical truth to every area of life, responsibility for sharing the Christian faith, and responsible church membership.[1]

What Should We Be Doing?

Teach the youth in your church to go to media with a knowledge of what is there for them. In the case of television, some programs are worthwhile, others are not. Youth must learn the difference. With music, coach them to be selective listeners who are aware of the message of the lyrics, the rhythm, instrument selection, and even album cover art. In attending movies, assist them in seeing the danger of "putting up with" evil language, gratuitous violence, and meaningless sex just because "everyone else has seen it!"

Help teens talk about what they are watching on television, hearing on records, and enjoying at the movies. If you use media as a part of Christian education and discipleship program, the rule of thumb is to spend twice as long in meaningful dialogue about what has been seen or heard as the actual piece covered. For instance, if the movie is thirty minutes long, spend one hour in a learning setting for interpretation.

We involved in discipleship must take on the role of cultural resistance fighters. We must help our youth examine the messages they receive from the media. Will a certain toothpaste really make you a better kisser? Will a certain basketball shoe make you able to fly to the hoop? Will a beer-drinking habit help you be the life of the party surrounded by attractive people of the opposite sex? We must, at times, militantly take on the role of having to say that the media are filled with half-truths designed to move viewers in a singular direction with no regard for the rest of the viewers' lives. We have to let youth know that there are very few (if any) 30-second solutions to real life issues. This is an exhausting effort, and few people will take the time to really make a difference in youth's lives. We have to be careful and sometimes subtle in how we approach this task so that we do not turn off youth with our degrading of a major influence on their lives. Some suggest that talking back to the TV is healthy. If a commercial says that your family must take a vacation in a certain place, respond by saying, "We will decide where we will spend vacation!"

The media are part of youth culture, and for adults to question any medium is to assault a major portion of contemporary youth's life. Many adults have experienced the anger of youth when trying to help them understand the underlying message of a rock musician's life-style. Some relationships have been sacrificed as youth leaders have tried to point out the subtle erosion of values on television with each new ratings topper. Walk lightly, but carry a big stick. It is risky, even as parents, to call into question, ridicule, or critique these things that are so much a part of youth life.

Let's compare the media to a real live, flesh-and-blood teacher of your youth. If your youth were in a school or classroom, or had a teacher, curriculum, or textbook about which you had serious reservations, you probably would try to change the school, classroom, teacher, curriculum, or textbook. Would you allow a person in a position of discipleship leadership in your church or as a teacher in

the public/private schools your youth attend to promote the use of
alcohol, drugs, violence, and loose sexuality seen in most PG rated
movies nowadays? Would you allow a person to teach youth who
lives the life-style of some contemporary musicians and speaks with
the language heard on most prime time television series? But today's
media are just such "teachers."

What seems to have happened is that we have given over our
young people to these media without question. We would probably
all rather have had the parents of youth program them when they
were young children to be selective and intelligent users of media.
But they did not! and we are not!

Teens who watch television for four hours a day learn about a
world where no one every says no, where sex is loose and often
violent, and where sexual maturity is out of date. Today's television
message is, "Go for it NOW. Go for it again. Don't worry about
anything."

Just keep the illustration working in your mind. If a teacher were
insulting to a youth, you would speak up for the youth by speaking
to the teacher. You can speak to the "teachers" (TV, radio, and
records) by training your youth to use media wisely. You can address
the conflict that is in our world between following Christ in obedient
discipleship and being a mindless supporter of media.

Some people question the wisdom of limiting the media in church
and home. They feel this might create social misfits of youth and
children. Do not worry. Our society is so filled with media promotion
that teens in your youth group will hear the latest rock music, see
photos of the latest movie stars, and know the slang expressions with
television roots without ever being exposed to them in their home
and church settings. Our culture is so wrapped up in media messages
now that if one misses seeing the movie, it will be out on video
cassette very soon; it will be on television later. Commercials feature
stars; the theme song is in the record stores and on the radio. The
theme doll series marketed after a movie is a success will be coming
soon to a store in your area.

What are some specific actions parents and youth leaders can take?

We can read to our youth and encourage them to read for themselves. Youth leaders should not shy away from assignments involving reading as a part of the discipleship experience. We can help them discover the lost art of reading and hearing the spoken word. The Bible is our source of inspiration and authority. It is a written medium. God could have sent Christ to earth as Savior in the twentieth century where Jesus' messages and miracles could be video taped. We could have cassette tapes of the Sermon on the Mount. We could watch a documentary movie of His life that included interviews of Mary, Pilate, Lazarus, and Peter. But God chose to send His Son to a world where oral tradition and the written word were the method of transmission of information. We must continue the written/oral communication of spiritual values. Writing should be a part of youth's discipleship experience.

Discipleship for youth can counter the media's picture that immediate self-gratification is necessary and admirable with the thought that deferred gratification is valuable. Where television talks about now-ness, church can emphasize history. Where media emphasize visual/audio overstimulation, church can emphasize language as a foundational part of culture. Discipleship is a natural place to stress that the goal of life is not a single point in time but a lifelong process.

Examine media as you would any other potentially harmful part of youth culture. The media are not providing a balanced view of the foundations of life. Many times when intelligent, moral presentations are made, youth switch the messages off if they are not entertainingly presented.

Youth leaders can stress that life is not always entertaining, fast-paced, novel, exciting. They can help youth see the importance of history, continuity, tradition, and culture because media are not much interested in such things. Life as a disciple of Jesus Christ is not one great emotional media experience. It is not wall-to-wall good experiences and happy endings. Our ultimate victory is a future reality but this world is a place of sickness, death, and war.

We can elevate and nurture youth's feelings. Feelings are a portion of our lives that are at times controlled by the media. Adults are often confused when they observe youth laugh at the goriness of the megaviolence portrayed in horror/splatter films, but sit placidly while watching the six o'clock news report the tragedy of hundreds dying in a plane crash on the other side of the country. It is disheartening to see youth allow hard metal music to help them express their anger and aggression while intellectual stimulation in the absence of that music leaves them docile and bored. We may be faced with needing to downplay content in order to bring teens' feelings to the front. Discipleship groups must be safe places where feelings count. We must guide youth into group experiences where feelings are a major objective of the learning environment. We must teach our youth how to deal with feelings and express them in socially appropriate and God-honoring ways.

Improving interpersonal skills is another goal of training youth. Just a few years ago our culture brought people into situations in which they learned to live together humanly and humanely. Today the doors next door are bolted, and the neighbors might as well be hundreds of miles away rather than just over the fence.

Many family members no longer actively participate with each other and community activities but are passive observers of the pseudo life of comic families on the screen. If a Christian goal is that all people live and work together in harmony, we may have to give interpersonal skills development serious emphasis in our discipleship. The life of a witness, the life of a minister, the life of a servant is impossible without relating to others effectively. These actions are best performed in relationships that are frightening and even foreign to some of our youth. When a majority of youth's free time has been spent in listening and viewing music, movies, and television, they have developed few skills for relating to parents, peers, friends, extended family members, and neighbors.

Youth leaders must promote high-level thinking capabilities. Our youth have been taught well by the television "teacher" that if they sit still long enough and are quiet enough, the problem they are hearing and observing will be resolved in a few minutes without their worry or input. Discussions are like this in many discipleship groups. The teens wait out the leader because they know if they do not answer the authority figure will provide the answers before too long. They are conditioned to stall.

We, as disciplers and teachers, are conditioned to provide answers for a searching generation. We rarely allow a youth to struggle for very long with a question of major importance. Problem-solving thinking skills must be taught and encouraged in the church. Gone are the days when we could simplistically assume that if youth would memorize a few verses of Scripture and master the presentation of a system of confirmation and indoctrination we could turn them loose to be reproductive members of society and true missionaries of our faith. We have all seen youth in our groups who are churched but not educated, smart but not wise; they may have Bible facts but no common sense. The amount of facts we learn will not help us survive in the twenty-first century; we must be able to use that knowledge to make this planet a better place to live. That comes from the ability to think and reason.

Youth leaders need to nurture creativity and imagination. This is a major key to the advancement of the quality of life in which our youth will participate in the future, not the amount of knowledge they are able to gain. The media explosion has allowed us to pile up amounts of knowledge like never before. But creativity allows folk to dream of life improved, health extended, and reason stretched to the point that life is enhanced. By the time a child is five he or she has spent five thousand hours of playtime watching television. Disciplers must encourage, cultivate, and support the creative activities of youth.

Encouraging creativity in youth is not easy. Modern American society does not seem to value personal creativity. Television viewers and radio listeners watch and listen to copies of someone's creative ideas. Against such societal pressure, we have to teach our youth to be creative and use their imaginations.

Developing moral and ethical behavior is necessary for youth. We live in a world that applauds and exalts the unusual, the grotesque, and the bizarre in many areas. In such a world, youth need examples and instruction to grow morally and ethically strong. Though we cannot raise youth in an environment of all-positive role models for ethical and moral behavior, the small-group discipleship setting affords a good opportunity to surround youth with sinners struggling to live lives of moral accountability toward each other and God.

Note

1. From *Church Base Design 1986 Update,* II:51. © Copyright 1986 The Sunday School Board of the Southern Baptist Convention. All rights reserved.

15
Youth Discipleship and the Role of Parents
Jimmy Hester

"Mom, I know I made a decision to follow Christ when I was eight years old, but did I know what I was doing? Was I too young?"

"That testimony we heard at church tonight was so dramatic. It makes me wonder if my conversion really happened, or was I just fooling myself?"

"Dad, I don't agree with you. Sometimes your values and mine seem to be different. What's wrong with trying out some things to see if they are for me?"

"I don't want to go to church. I'm not sure I believe all those things they keep telling me about being a Christian. Just how am I supposed to know what God's will is? They never specifically tell me."

"Dad, your and Mom's faith seems so strong. What can I do to have such a faith?"

Teenagers raise questions about everything. That's a normal part of being an adolescent. Their declaration seems to be, "Don't accept anything you can't figure out for yourself." They appear to live by the Chinese proverb "I hear, and I forget; I see, and I remember; I do, and I understand."

Questions cover the whole realm of youth's experiences, especially their relationship to the adult world. They question the teachings of right and wrong, good and bad, what to do and what not to do. Teenagers want to know who they are and the meaning of life.

Spiritual matters that parents assume have been addressed and accepted by their teenagers now surface as doubts. Some parents feel their youth are throwing away the spiritual truths they were taught during the first twelve years of life.

The goal of Christian parenting is to love, affirm, discipline, and guide children to become mature, responsible, Christian adults. This goal is accomplished as parents guide sons and daughters to become responsive to God and responsible to God. The parenting of Samuel (1 Sam. 1:26-28; 3:1-10) is an example of this.

Jesus modeled leading someone to become self-disciplined and self-motivated as He related to the disciples. He encouraged the disciples faith by releasing them to carry on His mission. Parents are to encourage their teens' faith to carry on Christ's mission. That's what discipleship training in the home is all about.

Children are a gift from God. "Sons are a gift from the Lord and children a reward from him" (Ps. 127:3, NEB). Parents are responsible for God's good gift and are God's instruments in the child's life. Manoah's wife was informed by a man of God that she would conceive and give birth to a son. Manoah prayed, "If it please thee, O Lord, let the man of God whom thou didst send come again to tell us what we are to do with the boy who is born" (Judg. 13:8, NEB). Such is the prayer of many Christian parents.

"I want my teenager to love God and develop a strong faith."

"I want my teenager to have a lot of friends—friends who have the same values we are trying to teach at home."

"I want my teenager to study hard in school so her chances of getting a good job will be greater."

"I want my teenager to mature into a happy, productive adult."

These are all worthy goals for Christian parents. However, parents cannot wave a magic wand and expect such dreams to come true. Parenting is hard work. The task is great. The responsibility is awesome.

Parents are their children's primary teachers of religious values and the foremost examples of personal faith in God. Thus the home is the primary institution for discipleship training. God intended it to be that way from the beginning. Abraham was charged with making a covenant of God a matter of family heritage (Gen. 17:7-9). Deuteronomy 6:4-9, 20-25 has been called the commissioning charter for religious education in the home. The command is to create within the home an atmosphere that constantly portrays the religious beliefs and values of the parents. Deuteronomy 6:5-7 states the task clearly:

> You shall love the Lord your God with all your heart, and with all your soul, and with all your might. And these words which I command you this day shall be upon your heart; and you shall teach them diligently to your children, and shall talk of them when you sit in your house, and when you walk by the way, and when you lie down, and when you rise.

The task of rearing children in the nurture and admonition of the Lord cannot be accomplished apart from a parent's commitment to God. Parents must keep themselves attuned to the presence of God's Holy Spirit as well as to the worth and potential of their children. Genuine Christian parenting is impossible unless the parents experience the grace of God through Jesus Christ. And, if parents are to grow in their understanding and practice of Christian parenting, they must grow as Christians.

God holds parents responsible for sharing their faith with their children. This is frightening in a way, but can be challenging and rewarding. One way parents are rewarded is stated in Proverbs 22:6: "Teach a child how he should live, and he will remember it all his life" (GNB).

By the time children reach adolescence, much of their belief system is in place; at least the foundation has been established. Adolescence becomes a time to build the structure that will sit on the foundation, a structure composed of the teen's beliefs and values.

Where does the youth get the "building materials" to construct this structure of beliefs and values? Parents are a primary source. The parents who made the statements quoted earlier may not have known it but they were, in effect, stating their values as Christian parents. Values are usually defined as those things that are desirable or worthy of esteem for their own sake. Christian values are not objects or things; rather, they are the basic principles by which people live.

All parents teach values; however, some parents are more conscious than others of the values they teach. The most effective teaching of values occurs when parents have clearly identified their own values. Christian parents need to identify their values and chart a course that will help them teach their teenager the values they consider important. Proverbs 3:5-6 assures parents that they are not alone in this venture: "Trust in the Lord with all your heart, and do not rely on your own insight. In all your ways acknowledge him, and he will make straight your paths."

Through the developmental process, God provides tools to aid teenagers as they build belief and value structures. One tool is the increasing ability to think abstractly. An elementary school-age child may sing and understand, "Jesus loves me this I know, For the Bible tells me so," but children have difficulty understanding, "Jesus paid it all, All to Him I owe; Sin had left a crimson stain, He washed it white as snow." Teenagers begin to understand the deeper meaning of faith issues because of their ability to think in abstract terms. Therefore, they can grow in their understanding of Jesus' sacrifice on the cross.

Place this increasing ability to think abstractly beside the many physical and emotional changes taking place in a teenager's life and it becomes evident why parents need to be patient and understanding. But being patient and understanding does not mean that a parent cannot be intentional in seeing that her teenager is exposed to and given guidance in areas of faith development.

Let's define the role of the parent in youth discipleship training. The following terms and definitions paint a picture of a parent's role:

Example: one who serves as a pattern to be imitated or not to be imitated

Facilitator: one who makes something easier

Equipper: one who makes ready by appropriate provision

Enabler: one who provides the means or opportunity

Enricher: one who makes rich or richer

Encourager: one who inspires with courage, spirit, or hope

The meaning of these terms can be expressed in practical suggestions for parents that will help them convey Christian values to their teenagers. Consider the following ten suggestions.

Practical Suggestions for Parents

1. Acknowledge that children are gifts from God (see Ps. 127:3)

God's plan for His highest and best creation included placing children with parents so that parents will love and nurture the children until they can function on their own. God's plan also included children progressing through certain stages of development to reach the stage of functioning on their own. Parents should view each stage as a beautiful, significant part of development.

Consider the rose. From late winter when the tiny sprouts begin to break through the brown, dead-looking stalks until late spring when the first rose blooms, the rose bush progresses through stages. Each stage has a certain beauty all its own. There is beauty in the tiny sprout that suggests hope; there is beauty in the new foliage that suggests new life; there is beauty in the rosebud that suggests growth; and there is beauty in the full-blossomed rose that suggests completion.

A similar view can be taken of a child's development. The birth of a child is cause for celebration in the Christian home. As that new life develops, there is beauty in each stage. Yes, beauty is even evident in adolescence as youth make the transition from childhood to adulthood, from bud to blossom.

2. Dedicate teenagers to the Lord to be used in His service

A prayer for parents might be the prayer Hannah prayed, "Give [your child] to the Lord [for] all the days of his life" (1 Sam. 1:1). Recently a story was told about a teenager making a commitment to

mission service, having felt God's call to serve as a medical missionary. The youth's mother requested that the church pray for her son,
not that he might fulfill his calling but that he might reconsider what
he was about to do and not "mess up his life." She felt he would be
better in a local practice rather than running all over the world as a
missionary.

But dedicating teenagers to God involves more than their vocational calling. Parents need to dedicate their teenagers everyday in every
way to the Lord. From those major decisions such as vocation or
marriage partner to those routine daily tasks, parents need to allow
God to work in their teenagers' lives.

3. Make personal commitments to God
to grow as Christian parents

Churches may give parents opportunity to make this commitment
publicly in a worship service. Or, parents might consider responding
when the invitation is given, talking with their pastor in their home,
or making a private commitment.

As a parent's faith grows, so does his relationship with others,
especially family members. As the faith of a teenager grows, so does
his relationship with others, especially family members. That models
the great commandment given by Jesus when He said, " 'Love the
Lord your God with all your heart and with all your soul and with
all your mind.' This is the first and greatest commandment. And the
second is like it: 'Love your neighbor as yourself' " (Matt. 22:37-39,
NIV).

4. Identify values and convey these values
consistently in your behavior

If telling the truth is a value parents want their teenagers to have,
they should tell the truth consistently—not just when it's conven-
ient. If living within the boundaries of the law is a value they want
their teenagers to possess, they shouldn't drive seventy miles per
hour in a fifty-five miles per hour zone. If breaking down barriers and

stereotypes is something parents want their teenagers to do, they shouldn't tell jokes that degrade other cultures or groups of people.

Enough of the don'ts; what about some dos? Parents convey their values to their teenagers through positive as well as negative actions. Teenagers learn about ministry and caring for others as they see their parents minister to and care for others. Teenagers learn about God's unconditional love for them as they experience the unconditional love of their parents. Teenagers learn about sharing their faith with others as they see their parents attend church visitation or share their faith with someone visiting the family.

Teenagers ask many questions. Parents need to verbally express what their beliefs are. They should respond to their teenagers' questions honestly and openly, keeping the lines of communication open. This allows parents to express verbally what they have or will express through their actions.

5. Express love and acceptance to your teenagers

The first step in expressing love and acceptance is to be accessible. Jesus demonstrated accessibility to children when He said to the disciples "Let the little children come to me, and do not hinder them" (Mark 10:14, NIV). The Bible then says, "He took the children in his arms, put his hands on them and blessed them" (Mark 10:16, NIV). As parents demonstrate their accessibility to their teenagers, the teenagers will learn something of the Heavenly Father's willingness to be available.

Notice that Jesus blessed the children. In biblical times, parents blessed their children by passing on leadership responsibilities, possessions, and property. Genesis 48 records the account of Jacob blessing his two grandsons, Ephraim and Manasseh.

Parents can bless their teenagers today in many ways. Telling teenage sons or daughters that they are loved for just being who they are is a form of blessing. Passing on a treasured family momento that has deep personal meaning is a form of blessing. Whatever the form, blessing teenagers will go a long way in influencing their self-worth and expressing confidence in them and the hope parents have for their future.

As parents express their acceptance of their teenagers as persons, they will find that the teens can teach them about faith and spiritual matters, if parents are willing to learn from youth. Discipleship is the Christian's lifelong commitment to the person, teaching, and spirit of Jesus Christ. Life under Jesus' lordship involves progressive learning and growth in Christlikeness. As parents apply the biblical truth and share their faith, they model for their teenagers what it means to be a Christian. As teens learn, they will share with parents their Christian pilgrimages.

Love should be the attitude of a parent. By demonstrating unconditional love, parents can help their teenagers experience in a small way the kind of love the Heavenly Father has for them. Even when undesirable behaviors must be corrected, teenagers need to know their parents' love has not diminished. Parents might make Ephesians 5:1-2 their motto: "Be imitators of God, therefore, as dearly loved children and live a life of love, just as Christ loved us and gave himself up for us as a fragrant offering and sacrifice to God" (NIV).

6. View discipline as an ongoing process of helping your teenagers ultimately become self-controlled and self-disciplined

Discipline and discipleship come from the same root word. A disciple is a follower and learner. Jesus is often referred to in the New Testament as a teacher and His followers as disciples. This suggests that discipline and discipleship involve a teaching-learning relationship.

As parents discipline their teenagers, they should go beyond mere punishment to teach something about life and living. Proper discipline will help teenagers find more acceptable kinds of behavior and will teach them how to effectively incorporate such behaviors into their life-style.

Taking advantage of teachable moments is a good way to teach, sometimes before inappropriate behavior occurs. Teachable moments are usually associated with preschoolers. But teachable moments occur with teenagers too. Parents can share with their teenagers about God's standards simply by being sensitive to those times when teenagers refer to something that happened at school or with friends. Asking a simple question such as, "How did you feel about that?" may open the door for dealing with a spiritual matter a teen is questioning.

7. Pray daily for your teenager

Doubts, turmoil, and conflict are often necessary in developing faith. Teenagers experience all three. They need support from parents in all areas of life. Prayers lifted up on behalf of teenagers will go a long way in supporting them during these years of development. Remember Jesus' promise in Matthew 7:7: "Ask, and it will be given you; seek and you will find; knock, and it will be opened to you."

8. Parents should maintain family worship and Bible study in the home

These periods of worship should be times for both thanksgiving and problem solving. Parents should not use the time as an opportunity to "preach" sermons. Parents can allow teenagers to lead in the worship experience some times. They can be creative and practical with what is included in these times together. *Home Life* magazine offers an easy-to-follow weekly Bible study and daily worship guide. *Living with Teenagers* magazine offers a monthly feature designed specifically for parents and their teenagers called "Home Encounters with the Bible."

9. Parents should involve their teenagers in church activities

The church is a valuable asset to parents. Church leaders care for parents and their teenagers. Church leaders want to be a part of the discipleship process. Parents should attend church regularly with their youth. They need to discuss what goes on there and encourage their teenagers to be active in the youth activities of the church. Next to the home, the church is the most valuable resource for discipleship training.

**10. Parents should participate in events the
church offers to help them grow as a Christian parent**

Parents need to be sensitive to the many avenues of development they can take to become the best parents they can become. Church libraries contain many good books that offer information to parents of teenagers. *Living with Teenagers* is a quarterly magazine specifically for parents of teenagers that offers guidance and encouragement. Church Training conferences and classes on family issues offer opportunities to learn and share with other Christian parents. An example is the new Parenting by Grace course *Parenting by Grace: Discipline and Spiritual Growth.* Sunday School lessons on the family and mission and ministry opportunities through mission organizations are all a part of Christian parents growing in their faith and their ability to share that faith with their teenager.

What assurance do parents have that all or any of this will make a difference in their teenagers' lives? If Christian parents have done their work of providing spiritual guidance in the home and through the church, by example and direction, then they have every reason to believe that God will do His work through His Holy Spirit.

16
Youth Discipleship
and Life's Choices
Karen Dockrey

Who will I marry?
What job do I want?
How deeply will I be involved with Jesus?

The youth years include these and many other critical choices. They are critical because they determine the direction of the rest of youth's lives. Mate and vocation have earned the top ranking positions, but they are preceded by and composed of many smaller, yet no less important, choices. Youth choose:

- Friends and acquaintances
- Leisuretime activities
- How to spend their money
- The life-style they'll work toward
- Who they will date
- How they will solve problems
- Where they will turn in times of trouble

Each of these choices is heavily influenced by the youth's level of obedience to Jesus. We call this discipleship—learning to live our commitment to Jesus. Yet often youth don't even make the connection. Youth's actions demonstrate their feeling that "Jesus is for Sunday, and His will is for the big choices like college, marriage, and vocation. The rest of what I do matters little to Him." In reality, the day-to-day activities and choices are precisely what contribute to youth's ability to understand and obey Jesus. So how do we youth workers help them make the connection?

First we examine our teaching and separate the detrimental from the helpful. Too often we communicate Jesus' interest in youth's decisions as a kind of faith test: "Do you love Jesus enough to give up your happiness and go His way?" Rather than picturing Jesus as passively waiting for youth's decisions, let's present Him offering assistance to youth during their decision making. Jesus wants to listen to youth, to help them untangle their thoughts, to understand their struggles, and to guide them to decide what to do about them. Youth find great comfort and deepened commitment when they invite Jesus along on their decision journeys.

The key is *involvement*. Jesus wants to be involved with youth and wants them to be involved with Him. Involvement is the essence of discipleship—reread the definition on which this book is based:

> *Discipleship* is the Christian's lifelong commitment to the person, teaching, and spirit of Jesus Christ. Life under Jesus' Lordship involves progressive learning, growth in Christlikeness, application of biblical truth to every area of life, responsibility for sharing the Christian faith, and responsible church membership.[1]

Notice key words like "lifelong," "teaching," "Lordship," "progressive learning," "growth," and "application." These action words communicate a journey, a process, an evergrowing relationship. They depict the warm and trusting relationship with Jesus that we want for our youth. This relationship results in making decisions *with* Jesus, rather than choosing and then bringing those choices to Jesus for approval.

How can we guide youth toward this? Three avenues are especially clear: personal attention, opportunity for success, simulated decision making.

Personal Attention

Because each youth's decisions are unique, take time to listen, in casual situations as well as scheduled appointments. Keep these questions on the tip of your tongue to use whenever you're with youth:

- How are your relationships going?

- What was the best and worst about your week?
- What are your thoughts about college/career?
- If you could do anything for Jesus, what would it be?
- What problems are you facing now?
- What decisions are you making? What options do you see?
- How are things between you and God?

As you talk with youth in casual settings, you earn their trust for larger decision making. When you take their small choices seriously, they begin to recognize that Jesus does care about the daily details. They notice that the way they treat people in day-to-day relationships can glorify God as much as deciding which college to attend or which vocation to pursue. They learn to trust their dialogue with Jesus and begin to heed what they hear Him saying.

Lest you feel overwhelmed by the number of youth to whom you minister, realize that even a sentence of encouragement and a moment or two of concentrated listening can make the difference between youth trusting God's advice and shrugging Him off.

Opportunity for Success

As much as we as youth workers would like to influence our youth's decisions, only they can make their choices. We can prepare and equip them to choose by providing opportunity for success in smaller choices. As youth experience success, they begin to trust God's wisdom and find it easier to obey Him.

First notice ways youth are already making positive choices for God:

Shelley rallied around Susan when her mom died. Shelley spent time at Susan's house, listened to her talk, and made sure she got to youth events. Shelley's youth leader noticed her sensitivity and complemented her, "You know Shelley, you're loving like Jesus loves. That's what Christianity is all about." "It is?" replied Shelley. "I thought I was just being a friend."

This worker pointed out Shelley's success in day-to-day obedience. Shelley had always thought serving God meant going on a choir trip or becoming a missionary. She'd never connected faith choices with her daily life. She began to gain confidence in her ability to serve God and deepened her relationship with Him. She reached out more and more.

Alan developed quite a successful lawn-mowing business. Alan's Sunday School teacher noticed the amount on his envelope and complemented his commitment to tithing. She said he was an example to the other youth.

This teacher went on to explain that tithing is easiest when it becomes a habit early. She complemented Alan for seeing all money as God's money. Alan's pride in God intensified, and he continued to tithe as he made more money.

Second create opportunities for youth to succeed.

Rachel said very little during Bible studies, but Rachel's doodling was remarkable. Her leader asked what she liked to do best and discovered an interest in art. So the teacher asked Rachel to make a rebus for a Bible concentration game. Rachel arrived early with her illustration and slid it under the learning game. As her peers searched their Bibles to find the answers, Rachel beamed. She knew the answers because she had studied them to create the rebus. She certainly participated in Bible study that day!

Rachel discovered that she could contribute to Bible study through her art. She succeeded in Bible study which led to a deeper trust of God's Word. She'll more likely trust God's answers next time she looks for them.

Josh excelled in sports but also excelled in tantrums. When he bungled the ball, he became furious with himself and the rest of the team. When he made a mistake in class, he became disruptive. Though Josh's youth leader felt like throwing Josh out of the class or the game, he talked with him privately about his behavior, encouraged him to focus on his successes, and assured him that everyone failed from time to time. He persisted in affirming Josh's successes, while encouraging him to learn from his mistakes.

Gradually Josh succeeded in learning how to fail. He discovered that the other members of the youth group thought no less of him when he made a mistake, so he didn't have to put himself down so dramatically. Thankfully Josh's youth leader didn't throw him out. Josh is a pastor today.

Simulated Decision Making

The main problem with making life's choices well is that we have to make choices to learn how to make them well. And some of those choices will be wrong. If youth can make some of their wrong choices in simulated situations, perhaps they can learn to anticipate real life consequences without having to experience them. Many curricula and book stores provide ready-made simulations but don't hesitate to create your own:

Marriage Simulation

Arrange for mock marriages in which youth choose, marry, and raise a family with someone from the youth group. Be certain to debrief and evaluate the experiences. Let youth talk more than you do and avoid "I told you so!"

Variations are endless, but consider these elements:

- The mock couples volunteer for the experience.
- The couples find a job in the want ads for which they are presently qualified. They build a year's budget around the salary offered. Items that must be included are:
  —rent and utilities quoted for an actual apartment
  —groceries based on prices in your local stores
  —clothing
  —medical expenses
  —insurance (medical, life, auto)
  —car payment or alternate transportation
  —phone bill as quoted by the phone company
  —extras such as date money, televisions, furniture and spending money.
- The couples care for a child in some way. One group used raw eggs that had to be taken care of twenty-four hours a day. If the egg broke, cracked, or rotted they failed as parents. Two o'clock AM feedings were included.

- The couples solve mock problems presented by the leader, such as: one spouse gets a job in another city; both want to spend Christmas at their own parents' home; one wants to make a major purchase that the other says they can't afford.

Consequence Chains

"It's OK if you don't get caught" states a prevalent attitude about morality. But all actions have consequences whether one gets caught or not. Some of the consequences are pleasurable, some are painful. God's laws are designed to lead us toward the pleasure, not take it away. Recognizing consequences is one way to help youth trust God's Word.

- During Bible studies, help youth connect actions and consequences through such questions as: What would have happened if the person chose to obey God rather than disobey Him (or to disobey rather than obey)? What were the consequences of that action? What actions led up to this consequence?
- Create consequence chains from actions to their results. For example: If I take one drink, it will dull my reaction time. I'd probably make it home OK, but I would not be able to handle traffic and could damage my car, injure a person, or even kill someone.
- Create consequence chains that retrace complex problems to the sins that probably created them. For example: War is caused by a leader who wants to rule another country. The leader's desire to rule is caused by his need to be recognized. His desire to be recognized is caused by people who rejected him. This started when he was in grade school and no one would be his friend. Ask: How might we turn some of these situations around before they grow to worldwide problems?

Sample Situations

Though overused and sometimes misused, the case study remains a valuable teaching tool. Consider these variations on the case study approach.

- Let youth write their own case studies. Case studies become particularly powerful when the situations come from youth's own lives. Guide youth to anonymously write letters asking advice on a problem they or a friend face. Then shuffle the letters and redistribute them. Guide youth to give advice as God would give it. Read the letters and responses and discuss them as a group with questions like: How well do you think this advice will work? What obstacles will this person face when she follows this advice? Why are these obstacles worth it? What rewards will there be? What other advice would you give?

- Present case studies without clear-cut answers. As much as we'd like it to be otherwise, most of life's decisions are not black and white. Many times two right choices compete or suffering seems inevitable either way. For example:

  Nan's band competition and church mission project are on the same day. A band friend has asked about Christianity, and Nan thinks the bus ride will be the ideal time to talk in depth. But a child at the mission is looking forward to Nan's return.

- Dramatize two solutions to the case study: the way most youth would solve it; the way God recommends solving it. Discuss both solutions with such questions as: How are God's way and the popular way similar? Different? When is the popular way easy? When is God's way easy? Why does God's way bring a more lasting solution?

- Role play the situation with youth in roles they do not have. Examples: Let two youth be the parents while an adult leader plays the role of the teenager. Let youth play the role of the teacher, the church leader, the young sibling.

Youth ministers and adult youth leaders can work more directly with youth in the areas of personal attention, opportunity for success, and simulated decision making. However, when it comes to actual decision making, youth leaders have to become equippers.

Only the youth themselves can make the decisions that will affect them the rest of their lives.

Actual Decisions

Youth workers are often privileged to guide youth through actual life choices. This section provides brief suggestions for enhancing our guidance.

Salvation

Because the level of their commitment to God determines the direction of all youth's life choices, the initial decision youth make is whether they will become Christians. Studies indicate that a person who leaves the youth years without becoming a Christian will not likely become one. We can encourage youth's interest in Christ through:

- Bible study: Every Bible study is an evangelistic opportunity because every Bible passage demonstrates at least one aspect of the Christian life. Sometimes you'll offer an invitation. More often you'll highlight the advantages of living life with God.
- Peer testimonies: As an opening or closing to a youth session, invite several youth to share one sentence about why they're glad to be Christians. Examples: "I'm so thankful for someone who's been through every feeling I have." "I know I'll never be alone."
- Personal relationships: "What do you think about God?" "What are your thoughts about church?" "What do you see as the differences between Christians and non-Christians?" These and other questions provide avenues for youth to share their spiritual status and needs.

Dating/Marriage

Perhaps no person will impact a youth's life more deeply than the person he chooses to marry. Because we strive to please the one we love the most, a marriage partner helps determine actions, values, and attitudes. Most youth know this intellectually but fail to consider it until they feel serious about someone they're dating. Then most conceal potential incompatibility with, "We're in love, so we must be right for each other." Encourage youth to choose their dates and mates carefully in these ways:

Study dating as often as you study such important subjects as witnessing. Select approaches which encourage youth to voice and evaluate their viewpoints. As they talk about their ideas, they discover why God's ways make sense and become willing to obey them. Possibilities include:

- What personality characteristics do you most want in a marriage partner? Date people like your description.
- God's guidelines always point us toward happiness. Name five reasons people have sex before marriage. Defeat these reasons with reasons why waiting until marriage will make you happier.
- Name five reasons for dating only Christians and five dangers of dating non-Christians.
- List at least fifty different things a couple in our town can do on a date.
- List fifty things to do if you don't have a date on the weekend.
- How can you break up in the least painful way? How can you tell the time is right? What words should you use? Is it better in person or on the phone? Why should you avoid the avoidance technique?
- List the differences between love and infatuation.
- How can dating couples solve their problems positively? What's the difference between a normal problem and one that signals danger?

Teach relationship skills like communication, conflict solving, affirmation, encouragement, and honesty. We go to school for almost everything but what matters most: relationship building! Base your studies on Bible passages that exemplify God's relationship skills. Model the principles in your own life.

Lead a book study on dating or marriage. *Before You Marry* (Convention Press) and *Dating: Making Your Own Choices* (Broadman Press). are two possibilities.

Keep a file of articles, tapes, and pamphlets to distribute when opportunities arise. The Christian Life Commission (P. O. Box 25266, Nashville, TN 37202-5266) offers a "Christian Lifestyle for Youth" series which includes pamphlets on dating, marriage, and sex.

Encourage youth to make smart choices as they date. Agree that they are the only ones who can choose who to date and marry. Express your confidence in them both individually and in groups.

Vocation

Too often we create a false hierarchy of vocational commitment: Those who are intensely committed to God will become a pastor or church staff minister. The totally committed ones become foreign missionaries. But God needs workers in every profession. A person who might never enter a church can be won to Jesus by a fellow engineer.

Ways to provide opportunities for discovering God's vocation for each youth include:

- Mini-internships: Request help from the adults in your church. When youth express interest in a particular vocation, match them with an adult in that field. Suggest that the adults share how they serve God in their vocations, invite the youth to observe the work (if feasible), and discuss what they like most and least about their jobs. Encourage continuing friendships.
- Listening: Notice when youth excel in certain areas or express interest in certain vocations. Encourage them to share what they would like about that job, what they think the disadvantages would be, and how they think they can serve God through that job.
- Vocational Workshops: Prepare an evening during which committed Christians in several vocational fields will share for five to ten minutes on how they serve God in their professions. Decide whether to arrange the presentations to occur concur-

rently and youth select the ones they want to hear, or sequentially so all youth hear all presentations. Encourage younger youth as well as older youth to attend. This enables them to consider options and to plan accordingly.

- Printed Materials: The Career Support Section of the Baptist Sunday School Board (MSN 157a, 127 Ninth Avenue North, Nashville, TN 37234) offers a set of pamphlets called the "Vocational Guidelines Series." These detail various church occupations as well as guidelines for choosing a secular vocation. Keep these handy to give when youth ask questions. Distribute them to all youth by using them as a basis for a session or unit on choosing a vocation.
- College Information: Most colleges are delighted to offer printed materials, visiting speakers, and other information on the programs they offer.
- A Positive Attitude Toward Work: Many youth feel that the best jobs are those that require the least effort. Communicate that work done well can glorify God.

Life-style

As early as seventh grade, youth recognize the popular people and categorize everyone else in one of the other groups. The names of these other groups change from year to year and from geographical area to area. Samples include "jocks," "druggies," "brains," "airheads," "preppies," "punkers," "kickers," "nerds," "rednecks," and "geeks." Consciously or unconsciously, youth decide which group they will pursue. These life-style choices impact youth's identity and value formation, which influence adult life-styles. Daily situations at school force youth to decide: Is it more important to be myself or act the popular way? Will I take care of the body God has given me or abuse it to find acceptance with a certain group? Will people or possessions or positions take first place in my life?

Once again, these questions are variations of the central question: Will I live God's way or choose another way? Guide youth to consciously choose God's way through actions like these.

- Group youth with others from their school and direct them to draw the hierarchy at their schools. As they display their illustrations ask: Who's at the top? What are the popular people like? Who earns the most respect from peers? From teachers? Which people treat other people the best? Why is the way you treat people important? Which group would God recommend you joining?
- Read Ephesians 4:29. Ask: Why do we find it easy to rank people, to place some above others? What does God think about this? Why? Even though we know in our minds that all persons have value, we don't live that way. Why? How can we obey Ephesians 4:29 in our relationships with every person at school?
- What does each group at your school value? How do their actions demonstrate this? Which life-styles match Jesus' life-style?
- What really matters in life (God, people, friendships, family, being accepted for who you are)? How do youth at your school admit or deny what really matters?
- How can you live your beliefs at your school? Which friends will help you live your Christian faith? How can you help friends live their Christianity?
- If you and God sat down and talked together, what life-style would He recommend for you? What people would He like you to be close to? What attitudes, words, and actions would He most like to see in you?

Equip Youth Rather than Do It for Them

Whew! How can one youth worker do all this? The effort it takes to train youth to choose makes us want to just tell them what to do. But we cripple youth when we make their choices for them. The easier route seems to be to forbid all sin, to distribute pat answers, and to prevent struggle by deciding for youth. But youth grow closer to God and become more committed to living God's way when they make their own choices. They discover why sin is wrong, why God's answers make sense, and why the struggle leads to strength.

So along with parents, your pastor, and others who love youth, teach decision making skills such as:

- Evaluation
- Searching for input from the Bible and prayer
- Talking with mature Christians
- Thinking through consequences
- Weighing the pros and cons of each choice
- Recognizing that it's always worth it to obey God.

Youth must often do all these in a split second when friends invite them to help vandalize or when a date's hand moves a little too far. So practicing ahead is great preparation. Even when youth have more time, they'll decide better when they realize that through Jesus, they have the ability to make good choices.

Let youth know that Jesus is by their side to help them know what to decide and to empower them to do what they decide. Rather than letting life happen to them, youth can impact the world for Jesus through their choices.

Note

1. From *Church Base Design, 1986 Update,* II: 51. © Copyright 1986 The Sunday School Board of the Southern Baptist Convention. All rights reserved.

17
Discipleship Methods for Youth
Billy Becham

Introduction: Foundational Principles

Basic discipleship principles and spiritual growth objectives should be threaded throughout your entire youth ministry. Every activity, Bible study, or event should fit into your overall goal of evangelism and discipleship. A few foundational principles relate to most all discipleship methods. An effective discipleship ministry:

• *Is never accomplished by just one person.*—You cannot do it alone. Sure, you need to have the vision and coordinate it, but you must have a *team* (whether lay help or paid interns). Ephesians 4:11-12 makes it clear that your responsibility as a minister is to prepare and equip others to minister. God never intended for you and me to do it all. Training a team is not only the most effective and efficient way to minister but also provides the greatest opportunity of growth for others. Your top priority should be to concentrate on building a ministry team of a variety of ages and a variety of personalities.

• *Never happens fast.*—Usually what comes quickly seems to go quickly. The big, flashy, "Madison Avenue" approach to youth ministry isn't necessarily the most effective discipleship ministry. Events to draw numbers can be planned easily but to effectively mature believers requires more. You can't build a ministry team in a few short weeks. You can't turn out youth who are reproducing spiritually in a few short months. You can't build a truly effective discipleship program in a year and then leave. It takes planning, patience, persistence, and most of all longevity.

James Dobson shares a story his mother told him about the high school she attended in 1930. The school

> was located in a small Oklahoma town which had produced a series of terrible football teams. They usually lost the important games and were invariably clobbered by their arch rivals from a nearby community. . . .
>
> Finally, a wealthy oil producer decided to take matters in his own hands. He asked to speak to the team in the locker room after yet another devastating defeat. . . . This businessman proceeded to offer a new Ford to every boy on the team and to each coach if they would simply defeat their bitter rivals in the next game.
>
> For seven days, the boys ate, drank and breathed football. At night they dreamed about touchdowns. . . .
>
> Finally, the big night arrived and the team assembled in the locker room. . . . Then they ran onto the field and were demolished, 38 to zero. The team's exuberance did not translate into a single point. . . . Seven days of hoorah and whoop-de-do simply couldn't compensate for the players' lack of discipline and conditioning and practice and study.[1]

You see, no matter how badly you may want something, some things just can't be accomplished quickly. You don't become a winner in a week. You must take up your cross daily (Luke 9:23) in obedience and diligently pursue Christ in your own life and be patient as God develops your ministry. Concentrate on the depth, and allow God to take care of the breadth.

• *Won't all happen at the church building.*—It also won't all happen in the midst of your perfectly planned program. We too often try to plan God's anointing. David Walker, a friend of mine and pastor of First Baptist Church, San Antonio, says that he often gets on his knees in his study on Sunday morning and prays, "Oh God, please do something in our service this morning that is not in the bulletin." God will honor that kind of expectancy.

As I travel and teach Sunday School workshops, I often break the youth workers into groups and have each person tell which Sunday School teacher influenced him most as a young person and why. Ninety percent or more say that the influential teacher did more than just teach the class. That teacher spent time with the students outside of the Sunday School class. What a convicting discovery when the group realizes that the very thing that was most influential for them as youth is possibly the most lacking in their present ministry. The "planned program" isn't always where the greatest life change comes.

• *Won't be effective without prayer.*—"You can do more than pray *after* you have prayed, and you cannot do more than pray *until* you have prayed."[2] Dave Busby from Minneapolis, Minnesota, said, "If your program is larger than what you have time to fully *bathe* in prayer, then it's too large. You need to cut something out."[3] You notice how we try to plan God's blessing. Dave asked, "If God were to remove His hand from your ministry, how long would it be before you recognized it?" He went on to say, "It would be months before we would recognize it in our youth ministry because we already have it all *planned* out to do, with God or without Him." How convicting! We need not to get into the trap of thinking that we can rely on our plans but to count on God's power and annointing. "What are you attempting right now in your youth program that only God can do?"— something that there is no earthly reason why it should work; it will only come as a result of faith and miraculous answer to prayer. If you don't know of anything, you need to start searching for it because that is when God *moves.*

Without exception, throughout my ministry the greatest times God has moved can be directly traced to prayer. One of the most anointed and growing Bible studies I ever taught I soon realized was a direct result of prayer. I would not only pray for the individuals during the week but also would spend an hour or more in that very room, the night before, on my knees praying that God would move. And He did, week after week.

I recently was at a church that has one of the most successful youth discipleship ministers in the country, and I asked the youth minister, "What's your secret?" He responded, "I wish I had a secret. All I can tell you is it is God's moving in answer to our prayer. We bathe this ministry in prayer." I never cease to be amazed how quickly we forget the power we possess through prayer.

The great people of earth today are the people who pray. I do not mean those who talk about prayer; nor those who say they believe in prayer; nor yet those who can explain about prayer; but I mean those people who take time and pray. They have not time. It must be taken from something else. This something else is important. Very important, and pressing, but still less important and less pressing than prayer.[4]

What the Church needs to-day is not more machinery or better, not new organizations or more and novel methods, but men whom the Holy Ghost can use—men of prayer, men mighty in prayer. The Holy Ghost does not flow through methods, but through men. He does not come on machinery, but on men. He does not anoint plans, but men—men of prayer.[5]

• *Must be person oriented, not program oriented.*—As you decide upon the proper methods, keep your eye clearly focused upon the goal—the individual.

A *program-oriented* ministry often becomes an end in itself instead of the means to an end. It often caters to the students' *wants* instead of their needs. It produces numbers but no real depth and maturity. Its primary methods include entertainment, activity, pressure, persuasion, and guilt. It eventually leads the youth minister to frustration, stress, and burnout.[6]

The *person-oriented* ministry seeks to develop the individual in Christ (Col. 1:28). The focus is changed from programs to people. The three distinct parts are still present: the individual, the method, and the goal. The individual is not a faceless number but a unique soul with spiritual needs. In order to meet these needs, your methods must be individually tailored and often reevaluated and updated.[7]

Discipleship Through Worship

"Come let us bow down in worship." "Worship the Lord in the splendor of his holiness." (Pss. 95:6; 96:9, NIV). Most young people have a shallow comprehension of what true worship is, much less the biblical importance of it. Through effective discipling, young people develop a greater thirst for God, and worship becomes much more real and important to them. A symptom of this is often seen in where they sit in the worship services and how they act. You can tell a lot about the youth program and the effectiveness of discipleship in a church by merely participating in one worship service. When young people are eager to grow, they are usually sitting close to the front, listening attentively, and usually taking notes (not writing notes to each other).

Help the young people understand that worship is not for *spectators*. Real worship involves everyone as *participants*. Allow them to be a part of a variety of worship experiences, even outside of the normal "worship service." These may be planned or spontaneous. Young people often learn much about worship during retreats or camps.

Occasionally provide opportunity within the church for them to be worship leaders, ushers, and soloists or the choir. After certain youth outings, have youth share in one of the regular church services. Learn to involve young people more often in sharing their testimonies in a public worship setting. You must help them see the broad perspective of worship; true worship includes singing, serving, listening, praising, sharing, praying, and giving.

Certain activities or lessons can help youth understand this in a more personal way. Take prayer as an example. You need to provide opportunities for youth to experience some genuine heartfelt prayer times in small groups or one-to-one. They need to be a part of prayer times where people are on their knees, pleading before God that He intervene in a particular situation.

Let me give you an example. A few months ago a friend of mine, a youth minister in West Texas, called and shared about one of their ninth-grade girls who was really growing spiritually as a result of her discipleship training. She was to a point where she felt really burdened for her lost friends. During prayer times, when she would pray, she would weep as she would mention their names. This, of course, helped others understand the sincerity of her compassion for lost people and others began to pray for her witness. In the next few weeks, six of these friends accepted Christ. What fruit! And this was all rooted in an effective discipleship environment where prayer and worship were real.

Discipleship Through Bible Study

"Like newborn babies, crave pure spiritual milk, so that by it you may grow" (1 Peter 2:2, NIV).

Create Interest

It certainly would be wonderful if all Christian young people did "crave" pure spiritual teaching, but that, usually, is not the case.

We must create interest for Bible study in our Sunday School. One common technique is called "salting." Salt creates thirst. You salt your audience by doing skits, telling an interesting story, doing projects that involve the entire group, or listening to a current song. Then you draw the analogy to the biblical principles which you will be studying that day.

To be effective in keeping Sunday School interesting, you do not have to compromise; you don't even have to try to compete with the world. But you do have to be creative and prepared. I have a friend who is an eleventh-grade department director at a nearby church. Every year his department grows to be twice as large as any other in the Youth Division. A few visits can quickly help you understand why. Even though this man and his wife are what I would consider very reserved, they have learned to be extremely creative and often even do crazy things to salt their youth. It is a blast to participate in their Sunday School Department. They have made Bible study very interesting.

You can also tell that they are prepared. This obviously can't be pulled off by looking at the lesson for the first time on Saturday evening. To be effective in Bible teaching, you need to at least scan your lesson at the beginning of the week. (I usually try to scan mine on Sunday afternoon.) Then you have all week to find current events and experiences in your own life to relate to the lesson.

Equip Youth to Feed Themselves

A baby eventually must learn to feed herself. If you are to build disciples through your Sunday School, you must begin to equip youth to feed themselves. If you are to eventually lead them to be fishers of men, you can't catch all the fish for them but must teach them how to fish. Hebrews 5:11-14 warns Christians of the danger of being milk-fed like babies for too long.

As a child, I had the opportunity to visit Yellowstone National Park, and I still remember the area where people could drive their cars into the middle of groups of semiwild bears. They would crawl onto the cars, and people would feed them through their windows (which were rolled down just an inch or so). I was unusually interested to hear in the news a few years ago that, when the winter was so bad and cold that no forest rangers could get in the park, some of the bears had died. Of course, many assumed that those bears had frozen to death, but autopsy reports showed that the bears had starved. The bears had become so dependent on others to feed them that they had never really learned adequately how to feed themselves in the wild.

A time will come in the lives of our youth when you and I won't be there to help. Therefore, we must not only teach them the Bible studies each Sunday but also, little by little, help and encourage them in personal Bible study such as a daily quiet time, or doing a character study. Many churches have one young person share a brief quiet time testimony each Sunday during the opening assembly. In most places where this is occurring, the number of youth having a daily quiet time has tripled. A testimony from a peer is often more effective than anything a leader could say.

Show Genuine Concern

A common oversight of Sunday School teachers is to major on covering material and not taking enough time to really get to know the students. If a student tells you something he will be involved in during the week, be sure to ask him specifically about it the next Sunday. I remember well a lady who wasn't a teacher in my Sunday School Department, yet she still had a big impact on my life. She was the records keeper. Her nickname was Mamma Norris. She was exactly like a mother to us. She always showed a deep, genuine concern for each of us as individuals. Your interest, or lack of it, in your students is easily seen. Do you go where they work (to buy your gas, etc.)? Do you send them birthday cards? Do you go to their games and contests? Do you send them cards of encouragement? Do you ever call to check up on them?

Discipleship Through Training

Your training time may fall on Sunday evening, Wednesday evening, or possibly some other evening in the week. An important part of any balanced youth ministry is a discipleship emphasis during the weekly programming. The Church Training Department offers some tremendous materials, such as "DiscipleLife," to help you in coordinating this aspect of your ministry.

This training time may be done in large group or in small groups, or in a combination of the two. Leaders and youth should have a higher level of *commitment* to this part of the youth ministry. This is an excellent place to involve interns, lay teachers/leaders, and even youth themselves in leadership positions. You take a risk when you give the young people big responsibilities, but that's part of real training. I've often heard it said that "the greatest sin of youth ministry is doing something yourself that a student can do." Sure, the overall meeting may suffer if they make mistakes; but when you do it all yourself and do it right, what have you really accomplished?—not a whole lot of discipleship. Real discipleship usually progresses more like this: teacher does it—student observes, teacher does it—student helps, student does it—teacher helps, student does it—teacher observes. Discipleship training is not usually easy. Sometimes you have to be tough (Care enough to confront problem areas in their lives.).

Whatever else you do during this time, never forget the *basics*. Even as your group matures, students still need to share devotional insight, memory verses, witnessing experiences, and prayer requests for lost friends.

If this is a meeting lost youth may attend, you will need to be sure to present the gospel. Many successful youth ministers pass out an evaluation card at *all* of their meetings so participants can indicate if they received Christ or not. This practice also helps keep your focus clear for what you're really in existence for.

Discipleship Through Missions

"You will be my witnesses in Jerusalem, and in all Judea and Samaria, and to the ends of the earth" (Acts 1:8, NIV).

An important fact for young people to learn is that missions is just as important in their own schools as it is in a foreign country. They need to understand the ministry is their own "Jerusalem" as much as reaching the world. They need to be led to realize that they are missionaries in one of the greatest mission fields in the world—the public/private school system.

The old statements, "You may be the only sermon your friends ever hear," and "You may be the only Bible your friends ever read" are so true. In fact, for some youth, the only thing they know about Christianity is what they see in the lives of their church-going friends. I believe that there is someone who immediately thinks of your name when he hears the word *Christian*.

Youth groups seem to reach a definite turning point when they catch a vision for their school or community. Some groups struggle for years through program after program, yet never seem to turn that corner. Others seem to reach this point in a year or two. I'm convinced that when you approach "youth discipleship ministry" the proper way, and you're patient, this is possible in even the toughest situations.

And what an excitement it is to see the differences. Once one or two of the students discover the joy of leading a friend to Christ, it begins to spread. When this does happen, always be sure to incorporate public testimony into your programming. The excitement of a new convert seems to breed a contagious spirit in itself.

A youth ministry that reaches this point will still have its ups and downs, but there is a vast difference once students begin to grasp the importance not only of getting to know Christ, but also *making Him known*. Usually it's just a matter of time before their burden for lost souls spreads to the entire church.

In addition to being an effective personal witness, and then catching a vision for your community, a true indicator of a fruitful ministry is to look at how many youth are sensing a call into full-time Christian service or possibly even foreign missions ("ends of the earth"). We certainly don't need to push students to make commitments that aren't real, but we need to continually provide an environment and bring in special speakers who might encourage such decisions.

Discipleship Through Music

At one time most of the very successful youth ministries were built around a strong youth music program. In many cases, this is still true today, and often this is done very effectively. If that is the case, it is even more important that discipleship be incorporated into the music program.

One of the most important concepts that the young people need to understand is the scriptural importance of music in worship and singing true praise to God. Whether a person sings well or not, as she grows spiritually she probably will find increasing joy in singing to the Lord. When you find people who are growing spiritually, you will always find people who love to sing about their love for God.

Many youth choirs are subdivided into smaller accountability groups or teams with one person given responsibility as a leader. Thus the music director can pour his life and time mainly into the leaders, and they can, in turn, minister to their groups.

The youth themselves need to have input in discussing various evangelistic projects their choir can be involved in, in their community. They can also have share times and prayer groups to encourage and support one another.

Other discipling opportunities that may be involved with music are puppet teams, sound crews, multimedia teams, and so forth. These types of situations warrant themselves well to disciplining and building relationships.

DiscipleLife Celebration, developed by the Sunday School Board's Church Training Department, is a unique plan coordinating on a weekly basis, youth choir, snack supper, youth discipleship groups, worship, and after church fellowship around a central theme. Weekly suggestions appear quarterly in *equipping youth* magazine.

Discipleship Through Retreats

The greatest life change often comes about during or as the result of a retreat, camp, or "Disciple Now" experience. The more fast paced our world becomes, the more important times of "retreat" are going to be. It is very healthy to get away from the daily pressures and allow God to work.

A weakness of these events is that sometimes we build them around high-pressure evangelistic appeals and emotionalism. That is a mistake. Such structure often explains why students bounce from the emotional high of one camp to the next with little maturing in between. These events need to be built on solid commitment times and never should be an end in themselves. Events should be the spark or the *beginning* of a *process* of discipleship.

Camps or retreats are excellent places to kick off new discipleship groups or families that will continue when participants return home. In planning events such as these, enough lay-leadership teams are needed to provide one-on-one time with each student. That is where some of the most exciting things happen and where young people really open up.

Discipleship Through Recreation

One big misconception about discipleship is that it all has to be done in a structured week-to-week setting. Some of the most effective discipling is done in much less formal settings (such as recreation). These could be in a family life center or in recreational events that are organized by your church, or even in your own personal recreation. (I used to jog on a high school track in the evenings and had the privilege of leading several athletes to the Lord and discipling them.)

An effective church recreation program is excellent for evangelism. It provides an opportunity to reach many people who might not be reachable any other way. The objective of evangelism needs to be strong, or it will end up fading into the background and you'll find yourself striving for winning teams (athletic ability) but miss the mark spiritually (1 Tim. 4:8).

Remember the goal: not buildings, not programs, not good teams, but *individuals conformed to the image of Christ.*

Discipleship Through Special Youth Events

Years ago, youth ministry seemed to be largely made up of fun and games. In recent years, it almost seems as though the pendulum has swung the other way. Now the more serious, spiritual side of youth ministry seems to be receiving a lot of attention, almost to the exclusion of fun and games. Our spiritual objectives should be first, but they must include special events where the gospel can be presented in a culturally relevant manner. Just telling your youth to all bring a friend to next week's Bible study probably won't be a successful way to reach more youth.

There are a variety of ways of meeting this need. Some churches offer a fun-filled Wednesday evening program with a lot of hype, games, and multimedia, and then have a time when the gospel is presented. This is excellent if you have a developed ministry team to help you coordinate it each week. Many churches don't have the resources to enable them to do that every week. Across the country, an increasing number of youth ministries are "networking" to do large evangelistic events (maybe once per month). This enables churches to pool their resources and bring in personalities who can attract a number of lost students. This usually works best if it is done at a neutral location, such as a high school. (Last year in our area we had twenty-seven churches involved in ours, which we call "Off Campus.")

Discipleship Through Creative Methods

You can disciple in the midst of almost anything you do at home, at work, at play if you're just conscious of it. Remember, the essence of discipleship is *relationships.* Get out where the students are. If the

204 Handbook for Youth Discipleship

campuses are closed to you as a youth minister, think of creative ways to be accepted on campus, such as taking pictures or substitute teaching. You can always reach the campuses through your student leaders. Learn to take a student with you on campus whenever possible. Have them in your home. Encourage your teachers and parents in discipling others.

Make sure you are incorporating an effective follow-up plan for your new converts. Lack of follow-up is probably the greatest void in our churches today, and it is devastating to a discipleship program. Involve older youth in ministering to younger youth whenever possible. Perhaps allow mature high school and college students to be sponsors at junior high outings or camps.

Don't make excuses! It is easy to excuse getting serious about your youth discipleship program. But I rarely hear a good one. You may say: If only I had: interns, more money, better buildings or a recreation center, more youth, more mature youth, more education or training, or more committed parents. None of these are really good reasons for not being serious about youth discipleship. All you need to do is get on your knees and get *started.* With God's help you can overcome any obstacle (Matt. 19:26).

Notes

1. James Dobson, *Emotions: Can You Trust Them* (New York: Bantan Books, Inc., 1982), pp. 1-2.

2. S.D. Paul E. Billheimer, *Destined for the Throne* (Fort Washington, Penn: Christian Literature Crusade, 1975), p. 51.

3. Dave Busby, "The Active Presence of God in Your Ministry," South Central Regional Network Conference, Arlington, Tex, 6-7 Nov. 1984. Recorded by Student Discipleship Ministries, Burleson, Tex., 6-7 Nov. 1984.

4. Rusty Rustenbach, "Toward a Life of Greater Power," *Discipleship Journal,* 1 Sept. 1986, p. 14.

5. E. M. Bounds, *Power Through Prayer* (Chicago, Il.: Moody Press), p. 8.

6. Pat Hurley, *Penetrating the Magic Bubble,* (Wheaton, Il.: Victor Books, 1980), p. 12.

7. Ibid., p. 17.

18

A Six-year Youth Discipleship Program
Clyde Hall

Youth leaders who take seriously the mandate of equipping the saints for the work of ministry (Eph. 4:11-12) will realize the importance of long-range planning. As in any move that is of major consequence, a great deal of prayer, preparation, and planning must go into the development and implementation of a youth discipleship program in a church. Consider a six-year youth discipleship program.

Youth are only youth for six years. Rather than plan for youth a week or month or even a year at a time, why not think in broad terms about a youth discipleship program that will span the six years youth will be in your program? What are your objectives for your youth discipleship ministry? your goals? your strategies? your annual plan? your plans for next month? next week?

What Is Youth Discipleship?

Youth discipleship is defined as "the Christian's lifelong commitment to the person, teaching, and spirit of Jesus Christ. Life under Jesus' Lordship involves progressive learning, growth in Christlikeness, application of biblical truth to every area of life, responsibility for sharing the Christian faith, and responsible church membership."[1]

This definition of discipleship suggests that discipleship training is for *all* Christian youth, that is for youth who are at various stages of Christian growth and maturity. It is for youth in a church who give evidence that they are serious about studing God's Word and following the example and teachings of Jesus, as well as, those youth who seem to be there only for fellowship.

The definition also suggests a lifelong commitment to a process. Discipleship isn't instant! It's not something that can be accomplished in a weekend. Some youth leaders have been heard to say, "We discipled our youth last weekend." This is not the type of discipleship we are talking about. The discipleship described in this definition requires daily commitment. It is never finished. It is lifelong!

Another fact in the definition is its focus on evangelism. Christians are expected to share their faith. Discipleship and evangelism are inseparable. You cannot have biblical discipleship without evangelism, and you cannot have biblical evangelism without discipleship.

This definition also points to the fact that discipleship is best expressed through a New Testament church. Discipleship that focuses only inward and not outward and does not direct personal expression of faith through a New Testament church is not complete biblical discipleship.

Many youth are exposed to discipleship teachings and discipleship disciplines before they become Christians. However, their lifelong discipleship journey begins only after they have made a commitment to the person, teaching, and spirit of Jesus Christ. All youth need to continually have opportunities to make discoveries about the Christian faith and the Christian life, before and after their commitment to Jesus Christ.

Determine Needs of Youth

Determining the needs of youth is no easy task! However, attempts need to be made. Have you ever asked a group of youth, "What do you want to study?" If so, you probably received negative reactions. Youth today are not too excited about the word *study* with all its implications. Maybe you should have asked, "What do you want to know about the Christian life? about God? about the Bible?" Youth need adults to guide them in their choices of study experiences at church. How can adults help you discover their needs for Christian growth?

One way adults can help youth with choices is through the use of a resource entitled *Shared Ministry*. *Shared Ministry* provides a self-study process for individual churches to access their strengths and weaknesses and to determine where they are and where they want to go in youth ministry. *Shared Ministry* can help a church identify its youth ministry priority areas and long-range youth ministry goals and objectives, including the goals and objectives of youth discipleship. *Shared Ministry* is a process based on the belief that when Christians share their understandings of what youth ministry ought to be, their vision becomes broader and clearer. The success of youth ministry is so vital that every now and then it is wise to collect, in a systematic, orderly way, the many different views people have of youth ministry. In this way you can make use of many minds to help you dream about what your youth ministry might be and to plan for the future.

Through use of the shared ministry process, you can:

1. Discover whether adults know youth's goals as well as they think.

2. Know whether your present youth work is producing the kind of results you wish.

3. Find new directions for ministry with and among your own youth.[2]

Another way to determine needs is to think about your youth individually. How are they changing physically, mentally, socially, emotionally, and spiritually? Consider the influences on their lives at home, in school, at church, and in your community. Do these influences affect their spiritual growth? Make notes!

Complete the Needs Checklist which is related to the youth in your church and their needs for discipleship development.

Steps in Planning A Youth Discipleship Program

Richard Ross has suggested eight planning steps for youth ministry which are appropriate in planning a youth discipleship program:

Needs Checklist[3]

Check the needs in the left column which are characteristic of the youth with whom you work. Then, note in the right column a discipleship training goal which speaks to that need.

Needs	Discipleship Goals
☐ to be accepted by other youth	● Identify oneself as a member of a fellowship of Christian believers, who are to support and care for one another.
☐ to set a vocational goal	● Analyze vocational interests and preparation as they relate to Christian ministry, considering the possibility of church-related/missions careers.
☐ to date	● Apply qualities of healthy, Christian friendship to special relationships with both sexes.
☐ to feel God's presence	● Demonstrate by establishing a personal, daily quiet time that discipleship in one's life involves Bible study, prayer, and continual spiritual growth.
☐ to understand why people get sick and die	● Understand that God cares even though illness, suffering, and death occur.
☐ to feel good about self	● Recognize the positive worth of oneself and that success and failure are experienced by all persons.
☐ to participate in physical exercise	● Make positive responses to changes that are taking place—physical, spiritual, emotional, social, mental.
☐ to feel God's love	● Apply God's forgiveness to oneself and others.
☐ to develop self-discipline	● Apply time management principles in keeping with Christian commitment.
☐ to pray meaningfully	● Evaluate the benefits of various forms of prayer.
☐ to trust God	● Profess or affirm one's faith in God through Jesus Christ.
☐ to care for other people	● Accept other persons as worthy.

1. *Look realistically at the way things are.* Evaluate your youth discipleship program by writing down the strengths and the weaknesses.

2. *Indicate several priority areas you would like to work on this year and the following five years.* Study your strengths and weaknesses. Write down the strengths you want maintained and the major weaknesses that need improvement.

3. *Determine the goals you would like to accomplish this year and the next five years.* Consider your priorities and your church's goals. Then write your youth discipleship goals in clear, concise, short sentences.

4. *Make a list of possible activities to be considered to help achieve each goal.* Brainstorm! That is, without evaluation list all the possible actions you might take to achieve each goal.

5. *Develop a tentative twelve-month and six-year youth discipleship calendar.* Build your calendar around your youth discipleship goals and priorities and in cooperation with the youth events planned and proposed by other church program organizations.

6. *Share tentative calendars with representative youth teachers, parents of youth, youth, and church staff members.* Seek feedback. Be open to suggestions.

7. *Rework your youth discipleship calendars after evaluating feedback.* Develop an annual youth discipleship budget, and propose any major expenditures for the following years.

8. *Prepare a planning sheet for each major event on the calendar.* Plan specifically for the events on the annual calendar and generally for the following five years. Begin by listing every action that needs to take place for the event to be a success, estimate how many weeks before the event each action should be performed, and determine in what week of the year each action should be performed.[4]

In thinking about your church's discipleship training program for youth, consider two types of goals: personal spiritual growth and numerical growth. Look at the Needs Checklist. Study the needs you have checked and the discipleship goals which relate to them. Determine the needs—goals that must be dealt with this year and the goals that can be dealt with within the next five years. Prioritize these goals. Keep in mind that some goals need to be set for next year, some for the year after, and so on. You should not try to accomplish all your goals in one year. Set only those goals you can realistically accomplish in one year. Plan now to accomplish other goals within the next five years.

A Youth Discipleship Taxonomy

A six-year youth discipleship program can be developed from a comprehensive listing of objectives based on the discipleship needs of youth. This listing of objectives is called a youth discipleship taxonomy.

"This taxonomy is a systematic classification of discipleship learning objectives for grades seven to twelve that are sequential and cumulative. Each stage of discipleship (Commitment, Community, Calling, Covenant, Competency, and Commissioning) is dependant upon the one before it. Therefore these sequential steps are cumulative. For example, step one is implied in all other steps.

"Each learning objective is scripturally based and reflects the needs of youth. These objectives, basic to a youth's discipleship development, grow out of the study areas—discipleship and personal ministry, Christian theology and Baptist doctrine, Christian ethics, Christian history, and church polity and organization."[5] This taxonomy is the basic tool from which the Southern Baptist youth discipleship program is developed. The discipleship goals on the Needs Checklist are selected statements taken from the youth discipleship taxonomy. Youth discipleship materials are then developed to accomplish these discipleship goals in the lives of youth over a six-year period.

The youth discipleship taxonomy gives purpose and direction for planning a six-year youth discipleship program in a church. It can be used to indicate where you have been (evaluations) and where you want to go (annual and long-range planning). The taxonomy is the foundation for youth discipleship strategies.

Three Youth Discipleship Strategies

The learning objectives of the Youth Discipleship Taxonomy can be accomplished through DiscipleLife. DiscipleLife is a Southern

Baptist growth plan for implementing youth discipleship development in a church. The plan will work with minor adaptations in any evangelical church. DiscipleLife brings together the curriculum, adult leaders of youth, and youth to cause the learning identified in the taxonomy to take place.

The three strategies through which the youth discipleship taxonomy can be expressed are:

1. *DiscipleLife Celebration* is a weekly, Sunday night discipleship event, coordinating choir rehearsal, snack supper, training, worship, and fellowship around the study theme of the youth discipleship group. Over a six-year period, most of the learning objectives in the taxonomy will be studied in periodicals such as: *Youth Alive, The Youth Disciple* and *Baptist Youth.* Coordination suggestions for DiscipleLife Celebration appear quarterly in *equipping youth.* DiscipleLife Celebration is for *all* youth.

2. *DiscipleLife Centers* are groupings of short-term and individual courses for youth around a subject area. Courses may be grouped in the following subject areas: Christian doctrine, discipleship-evangelism, ethical issues, family life, leadership, personal ministry, and stewardship. The Leadership DiscipleLife Center includes experimental projects such as: Youth Week, Youth Bible Drill, Youth Speakers' Tournament, and Youth Apprenticeship. The DiscipleLife Centers are usually implemented on weekdays, at camps and on retreats. DiscipleLife Centers are for *all* youth.

3. *DiscipleYouth* is an in-depth, fifty-two week, discipleship—evangelism process for youth. Through it, youth learn Christian skills and develop spiritual disciplines that are lifelong. They learn to use "tools" for spiritual growth that will help them for the rest of their lives. The DiscipleYouth process is expressed through two twenty-six week kits: *DiscipleYouth I Kit* and *DiscipleYouth II Kit,* which are not necessarily conducted in sequence. That is, DiscipleYouth I may be conducted and DiscipleYouth II may not be conducted until a year or more later, after a youth has thoroughly practiced the skills learned in DiscipleYouth I.

DiscipleYouth is for the church who has only one youth committed to in-depth discipleship-evangelism training as well as the church who has many youth who have made this commitment. DiscipleYouth may be conducted individually, on a one-to-one basis, or in a small group setting (two to eight youth). DiscipleYouth is not for all youth. It is only for those youth who have made a commitment to in-depth discipleship-evangelism training.

A Suggested Six-Year Youth Discipleship Program

Plan a six-year youth discipleship program based on the needs of your youth. The first year should be planned in detail. The other five years are planned in broad strokes, with more detailed plans appearing in the second and third years. After reviewing the needs of your youth each year, add to your plans. For example, you may determine that you will schedule weekly discipleship training for all youth and certain events each year, such as Youth Week, Summer Youth Celebration at Ridgecrest or Glorieta, a DiscipleNow Weekend, or retreat. Other events you might schedule every two or three years, such as a mission tour or a church or association youth camp.

As you plan, consider the following:

1. *Plan weekly discipleship training for all youth.* Select a curriculum that will provide a balanced course of study, for example, DiscipleLife Celebration.

2. *Plan weekly and annual short-term discipleship training for all youth.* Knowing what subject areas you will be dealing with each month in your weekly curriculum, select other subject areas for special weekday activities and retreats that will supplement the basic discipleship training provided through the continuing curriculum, for example DiscipleLife Centers. (See resources.)

3. *Plan special in-depth discipleship training for a select group of youth.* Provide opportunity once or twice a year for all youth to choose an in-depth study of discipleship evangelism, for example, DiscipleYouth.

See the six-month example of a six-year youth discipleship program. This example includes all three strategies of DiscipleLife: DiscipleLife Celebration, DiscipleLife Centers, and DiscipleYouth. For

A SAMPLE OF A SIX-YEAR PLAN

Year	October	November	December
1	Begin Youth Bible Drill/Youth Speakers' Tournament Weekday Study: Stewardship	Revival Weekday Study: Foreign Mission	
	Weekly Discipleship Training For All Youth Using Dated Periodicals:		
	Doctrine of God	Doctrine of the Bible	Early Baptist Missions
2	Weekday Study: Stewardship	Weekday Study: Foreign Mission	
	Weekly Discipleship Training For All Youth Using Dated Periodicals:		Foreign Missions 1845-1900
	Doctrine of Christ	Doctrine of Man	
3	Begin Youth Bible Drill/Youth Speakers' Tournament Weekday Study: Stewardship	Weekday Study: Foreign Mission	
	Weekly Discipleship Training For All Youth Using Dated Periodicals		
	Doctrine of Salvation	Doctrine of the Church	Home Missions 1845-1882
4	Begin Youth Bible Drill/Youth Speakers' Tournament Weekday Study: Stewardship	Weekday Study: Foreign Mission	
	Weekly Discipleship Training For All Youth Using Dated Periodicals		
	Doctrine of the Holy Spirit	God's Purpose of Grace	New Life through New Churches
5	Begin Youth Bible Drill/Youth Speakers' Tournament Weekday Study: Stewardship	Weekday Study: Foreign Mission	
	Weekly Discipleship Training For All Youth Using Dated Periodicals		
	Baptist Doctrinal Distinctives	Doctrine of the Kingdom	Foreign Missions 1900-1960
6	Begin Youth Bible Drill/Youth Speakers' Tournament Weekday Study: Stewardship	Weekday Study: Foreign Mission	
	Weekly Discipleship Training For All Youth Using Dated Periodicals		
	Old Testament Theology	New Testament Theology	Home Missions 1882-1968

January	February	March
DiscipleNow Weekend Weekday Study: Cop Out, Conform or Commit	Begin DiscipleYouth Weekday Study: Meaningful Moments with God	Youth Week Theme: Commitment-Foundation for Service Youth Retreat Weekday Study: Witness Training
Weekly Discipleship Training For All Youth Using Dated Periodicals		
Principles for Christian Living	Ancient Christianity	Called to Discipleship and Ministry
DiscipleNow Weekend Weekday Study:	Begin DiscipleYouth Weekday Study:	Youth Week Theme: Community—My Serving Family Youth Retreat:
Weekly Discipleship Training For All Youth Using Dated Periodicals		
Orientation to Christian Ethics	Medieval Christianity	Spiritual Gifts
DiscipleNow Weekend Weekday Study: Learning and Serving Workbook	Begin DiscipleYouth Weekday Study: Before You Marry	Youth Week Theme: Calling—To a Life of Service Youth Retreat: God's Will Weekday Study:
Weekly Discipleship Training For All Youth Using Dated Periodicals		
Stewardship of Life	The Reformation	How to Study the Bible
DiscipleNow Weekend Weekday Study:	Begin DiscipleYouth Weekday Study:	Youth Week Theme: Covenant—A Costly Life-Style Youth Retreat: Weekday Study:
Weekly Discipleship Training For All Youth Using Dated Periodicals		
Fruit of the Spirit	Modern Christianity	Developing Your Prayer Life
DiscipleNow Weekend Weekday Study: "Our Father . . ."	Begin DiscipleYouth Weekday Study: The Great Adventure	Youth Week Theme: Competence—My Ability to Serve Youth Retreat: Weekday Study:
Weekly Discipleship Training For All Youth Using Dated Periodicals		
Determining My Values	History of the Great Awakening	Discovering God's Will
DiscipleNow Weekend Weekday Study: Survival Kit	Begin DiscipleYouth Weekday Study: Deepening Discipleship	Youth Week Theme: Commissioning— Direction for Service Youth Retreat: All Times Are God's Seasons
Weekly Discipleship Training For All Youth Using Dated Periodicals		
Interpersonal Relationships	Major Christian Movements	Developing Witnessing Skills

a twelve-month model, write: Youth Section, Church Training Department, 127 9th Avenue, North, Nashville, TN 37234.

Notes

1. From *Church Base Design 1986 Update,* pp. II-51. © Copyright 1986 The Sunday School Board of the Southern Baptist Convention. All rights reserved.

2. From *Shared Ministry Administrative Manual* in *Shared Ministry,* p. 4. © Copyright 1982 The Sunday School Board of the Southern Baptist Convention. All rights reserved.

3. Roy T. Edgemon, Comp., *Discipleship Training: A Church Training Manual* (Nashville: Convention Press, 1986), p. 40.

4. Adapted from Richard Ross, comp., *Youth Ministry Planbook 3,* (Nashville: Convention Press, 1985), pp. 25-32.

5. R. Clyde Hall, Jr., "The Hallmark," *equipping youth* (October-December 1985): 4.

19
Administering
a Youth Discipleship Program
Sam House

Every job starts by deciding where, when, and how to begin. Bread baker or brain surgeon, most workers choose a starting point with an eye to what could result. That decision to start determines what will or won't happen. Youth ministry is no different. The commitments and goals of the leaders will affect the direction of any youth discipleship program. However, neither the strongest commitments nor the worthiest goals can help a discipleship program that is never started.

Dream

Dreams have a special kind of power. They can make things happen. In the Old Testament, Joseph's years of slavery began with a dream that angered his brothers enough to make them plot to sell Joseph and fake his death. Interpreting dreams for prisoners in Egypt brought Joseph to the attention of the pharaoh. Explaining the ruler's dreams placed him on a fast track to power and wealth. It also brought him the opportunity to save the Egyptians and his family from starvation. Dreams shaped Joseph's whole life. Dreams can also shape an inspired youth ministry.

I have often said that success in youth ministry comes ten years after that ministry. What young adults are doing for the cause of Christ can be greatly affected by the kind of discipleship opportunities they were given as teenagers. Some of the best discipleship training is provided by leaders who are willing to dream of shaping your lives into glowing testimonies for Christ. As in Joseph's experience, dreams can open our minds to limitless possibilities. Dreams can remind us of what we know. They can give us the chance to recognize what is in our hearts.

The goals that come from dreams can motivate us to plunge into the greatest challenges of our lives and ministries. Youth discipleship is such a challenge. To have the opportunity to be in God's hand, drawing out the potential of a young life like a potter working clay, is both staggering and exhilarating. Being one with the Holy Spirit in ministry also hallmarks the personal discipleship of any youth leader. It is truly one of the greatest growth experiences any Christian can have.

Dreams can begin by imaging. Focus on each of the youth with whom you have contact. Prayerfully inventory the gifts and abilities you are aware of in those young lives. Just as prayerfully, catalog their needs as you perceive them. Then imagine how God might use those capabilities and needs to shape each of those lives. Think of what God might accomplish through them in the next ten years. With all this in mind, consider anything and everything that you could influence, provide, and pray for in the near future through your ministry that would encourage the most complete expression of God's will for those youth.

Let your dreams turn inward. What did mature Christians provide for you as a teenager that influenced you toward following God's will? How did you come to understand the truths that guide your life now? What do you wish you had known between twelve and twenty that would have helped your spiritual growth ripen faster and yield more? What could you do to help that happen in the discipleship of youth you influence?

Continue dreaming, but dream about programs, places, experiences that could be arranged and experiences that could be encouraged. Imagine that you have every resource for crafting the finest youth discipleship program by which any Christian has ever been blessed. You serve a limitless God. Ask for a glimpse of God's vision, and model your reality after it.

Finally, the most luxurious dream of all: If you could go back six months, a year, or two years, what could you have done to move your vision of ministry forward? Do you wish you had organized a parents' assist team, scheduled retreats, arranged youth leadership opportunities, or thought through a whole year of ongoing discipleship activities and scheduled them? How about dreaming that you had trained some other adults in growing their own discipleship and aiding the growth of youth discipleship in your church? In this dream, you can also have the experience of being organized enough that you allowed time in every week to do nothing but be available to youth—either in the same place at the same time, each time, or out and able to follow up on individuals you need to contact.

Can you feel the adrenalin pumping? What you do for God has eternal consequences. The God you serve offers eternal possibilities. Don't be a self-limiting, self-centered, and self-reliant discipler of youth. Dream! Then, like Joseph, remember your dreams, share your dreams, and act on your dreams—by planning for them.

Plan

You may not have the ability to go back a year and plan what you wish you were doing now. However, you can look ahead and start the process of making some of your dreams come true. You could be the catalyst that makes your congregation so excited about the youth discipleship potential in your church that your youth ministry turns around. It could go off like a rocket, headed straight to the center of God's will!

The planning process starts before you call any meetings or print out any schedule sheets. With your dreams in mind, look at the overall programs in your church. Pose the question, What aspects of discipleship could be helped, even developed by existing Sunday School, missions, music, and evangelism programs in my church? What would need to be added to these programs or adjusted in the current youth program to make more discipleship opportunities available to the youth? Contact the leaders of those programs and stress that the value of their program areas could multiply if the programs were coordinated to be mutually supportive and focused.

Next schedule an informal time to confer with these leaders, preferably in someone's home. With the help of a relaxed atmosphere, lead them through the dream process. Allow them to share their feelings after you have finished and see if there isn't already a little new excitement over the prospects of a stronger, comprehensive, youth discipleship program. You may also feel that you have organized a wonderful tool called a youth council or committee.

Continue the planning process by inviting each person to go home and project the results of his or her dream survey onto the events proposed or waiting to be scheduled on the next year's church calendar. Now it is time to call a meeting and consider printing schedule sheets!

As you and your council provide the time and cooperation necessary for a visionary youth discipleship program, you can enjoy the benefits of an expanded ministry and pleasure of being united in the Spirit with the other leaders of youth in your church. That should make more energy available to implement the plans your dreams have helped create.

Implement

Suppose you do have one of the most comprehensive, well-planned, and thought-out youth discipleship programs ever conceived. What will happen if only some of the plans are put into effect? Only part of your program's potential to serve God will be reached. You will have been only partially responsible in carrying out your calling to minister to the youth in your church. To avoid some of the guilt and frustration that can plague every youth leader, plan your implementation as well. Just as you did with the planning, identify the resource persons and tools that will help assure you of having every opportunity you have hoped for in following your plans.

One way to keep things from slipping between the cracks is to get them off the floor and lined up on the shelf. Once your youth discipleship planning calendar is filled in, approved and blessed, spend a week or two lining up all the teachers, helpers, sponsors, peacekeepers, whatever you'll need for each even that is your responsibility. Compile a directory of all the parents of youth in your group and youth workers in other program organizations in your church. Leave space by each name to list the times you contact them to assist you and their responses. Enlist adult participants, both to help or just observe as your special guests, for every activity. Simply contacting adults on the assumption they have something to offer in furthering youth discipleship is a ministry in its self. Spiritually lost parents may even become more responsive to the gospel and supportive of their children's faith because of your willingness to involve them in even a small way. Include this directory in every mailing you send out. An informed pool of resource persons is a more responsive pool of resource persons.

Another tool that is essential is a record book of all the youth and youth prospects for your youth group. If you are not aware of what activities youth are supporting, you will never be aware of patterns and experiences that could be crucial crossroads in youths' discipleship. Every youth group has at least a couple of youth who show astonishing spiritual depth and growth. Your obligation as a leader is to disciple *every* believer. That means the occasional Sunday School-attending teen as well as the model Christian youth. Your command from Christ is to reach out to that socially backward or disruptive youth who once responded to an invitation to receive Christ but whose faith has never blossomed. These teens can be forgotten even faster than the refreshments for an overlooked fellowship if you don't create a safety net of records to catch them before they disappear. Comparing your records to the those of other youth program organizations will strengthen this net and help you be more sensitive to the discipleship needs and interest of all the youth.

To keep and attract all the assistance you will need, give visibility to the program. In letters, on postcards, through thank-yous in the weekly church bulletin, let people know what is happening, who is helping it happen, and why it is happening. Sharing the results of the discipleship dreams and goals of the youth program can minister to adults who may have forgotten the joy of a growing, closer walk with Christ.

Plan for periodic meetings with the council to iron out any overlaps and create opportunities to exchange gratitude and testimonies arising from the comprehensive discipleship program. Emphasize in your encouragement of each leader that all youth, even your local "celebrity" Christian teens, crave encouragement and affirmation. Stress the positive results of sending out postcards with a Scripture verse just to let youth know you are holding them up in prayer. Phone calls to parents of youth to report accomplishments or to thank parents for supporting their youth's Christian growth are essential. Such contacts create a warmer environment that encourages youth and parents alike to trust and involves youth leaders in ways that they can minister to these families.

As your implementation continues, your discipleship ministry will grow. So will the number and quality of the leaders. This should practically eliminate the frantic pace or burned-out depression that characterize so many youth ministry's approaches to youth discipleship. If that is the case, it will be because of three things:

1. You have stronger handles on your schedule and the youth discipleship program. You can act instead of react.
2. You share the responsibility and a vision for youth discipleship in your church with a number of committed Christian adults.
3. Orderliness in your ministry to others will allow more consistency in your own spiritual disciplines and growth.

Stronger handles, shared responsibility, and orderliness contribute to an attitude that welcomes those unexpected opportunities to be used of God in many situations. They can also replace a "have to" attitude toward youth discipleship ministry with a "get to" outlook. Your viewpoint makes the difference between administering a youth discipleship program that is exciting to you and one that is sheer drudgery. Perhaps most relieving of all is knowing that you possess the help and experience to evaluate how well the implementation carries the plans.

Evaluate

Evaluation provides the chance to make comparisons. How much of what you hoped for is there in what you have? Periodically gathering the council to compile and process questionnaires can be a great evaluation tool. To poll youth about their opinions, likes, and dislikes, both flatters and includes them. Requesting information on attitudes and reactions from parents can make them a little prouder of the years spent as somebody's mom or dad if you let them know you consider them experts on how they feel about their experiences. It can also make them less resentful and more supportive of any programs that seem to just be taking more time away from them as they watch their children race toward adulthood.

Just as important as evaluations from others is your own evaluation of the program. Does the current program resemble what you and the other leaders planned? Does it accomplish any of the goals born in your planning sessions? More importantly, does it resemble any of your dreams? Is it true to the vision for youth discipleship God gave you and the others? Are you growing? Are the other aspects of the program growing? What would you do differently if you had it to do over again?

Check your public relations. How does your pastor and church ministry staff feel about the youth discipleship program? Does the church office feel you are making too many demands on the clerical staff? Do some in the congregation believe that the youth program has interfered with the discipleship activities of other age groups? Be as objective and polite as possible in sincerely seeking information about problems.

Finally, how has the whole system of planning and implementing worked out? Is there a need for more records or files to help chart the progress of the youth? Think of any other person or program that should be represented on the youth council. Find out if there is information that is not reaching any of the leaders or parents. Most of all, share successes. Actively report on the spiritual fruit as well as personal blessings that have come from efforts in the youth discipleship program. Remember to always give God the credit for providing a ministry for you all to participate in. Thank Him for saving you and try to be as humble about your role in the program's accomplishments as you were about your role in coming to Christ for salvation. Bearing all this in mind, you may discover that it is time to revise.

Revise

The beauty of organization is that it generally makes things clearer. When something needs fixing or a counted-on resource doesn't materialize, it is a far easier thing to backtrack and regroup. With a plan you have been following, it is also easier to allow Christ to redeem the circumstance and show you how to grow from a new situation.

Even the best-laid plans can sometimes turn sour. The experiences leading up to a certain even may reveal needs in the schedule that no one anticipated. It may also show up things that no one needed. One of the greatest dilemmas in youth discipleship programming is that of "shoulds" versus "coulds." As twentieth-century Christians, we probably have more than our share of shoulds and coulds. Never before have so many had so much available to them about God and the Bible. At the same time, no other generation has ever been faced with so many choices of groups, methods, and thoughts. When it comes to youth discipleship, it is one thing to insist that all youth who want to grow spiritually must memorize a certain number of Scriptures. It is another to realize illiteracy and learning disabilities plague many adolescents. Resolving the difference between this "should" and a reality that keeps it from happening takes looking into some of the "coulds." Can all of the youth in your group memorize? Are Scripture memory cards the only tools you can provide them? Would pairing up kids and turning Scripture memory exercises into verbal activities include a youth who would have been excluded?

What about programming for youth who live in an age of working teens? Should discipleship activities always happen on a certain day of the week at a traditional time? Or, could the cause of Christ receive new opportunities if the schedule was expanded to reach more youth? Consider the baggage that you or other adult leaders may have brought with you from some of your collective pasts. Sometimes ideas or practices given us when we were youth stay with us like boxes of stuff we store but never use. Understanding why some youth have such strong feelings that may conflict with ours could be as simple as inspecting their baggage. You could recognize some of it. You should consider it. Pray for wisdom to never dilute the purity of the gospel by elevating what you want to the rank of God's will.

In planning with other adult leaders to achieve and administer a youth discipleship program through a youth council, evaluate the process and outcomes. Learning how to better understand these other committed leaders will not only strengthen the discipleship program but also can serve as a model of cooperation for the youth. The wonder of revision is that it attempts to improve on what you have. Such is the stuff dreams are made of.

Dream Again

The amazing power of God to redeem lives and circumstances is enough to meditate upon for some time. Add to that God's ability to bless and multiply those blessings and you have an equally mind-boggling sum. To have gained a vision, pursued, shared and begun to live it is an opportunity that only Christians can know to the fullest. Having survived one cycle of dreaming, planning, evaluating, and revising, it is time to dream again. Looking ahead to all that God could build upon your experience and service is almost overwhelming.

The contrast between God's potentiality and our limitedness is one that can sometimes bring depression even on the heels of victory. In the Book of 1 Kings, Elijah had experienced a miracle. It was no less than the miracle of a changed eternity we see in youth who turn to Christ, but definitely more spectacular to see. Fire had fallen from heaven to consume a sacrifice drenched with water. The false prophets of an idol lost their lives in the aftermath. For a man who had prayed for and received the impossible, it seems odd that Elijah panicked when Queen Jezebel threatened to kill him to avenge the death of her false prophets. But panic he did. Even after a supernatural experience, he felt alone, unprotected, and perhaps even betrayed by God who had not prevented this new danger. However, when Elijah had rested and searched his heart, he was open to God's new tasks. Within a few weeks he anointed two kings and a prophet. He learned that he only thought he was alone; God told him of seven thousand faithful believers. Not only did he remain safe from Jezebel, but within a few years, both she and her husband had received the horrible deaths their wicked lives had earned.

Administering an effective youth discipleship program will cause emotional wear and tear on anyone who works at it hard enough and long enough. But, sharing your dreams and knowing you took every reasonable step to plan for those dreams is a real source of satisfaction. The experience of evaluating the effectiveness of your plans is a blessing in itself. I use the word *blessing* because evaluation gives you the chance to make revisions. Through weighing and measuring the input and results of events, you may be able to redeem bad experiences and enlarge on good ones. With this exercise behind you, your dreams can grow. You can be confident that you have offered God your worthiest service. You can know better how to expand the sum of all the ministry opportunities He has given you.

At the same time, your well-planned, well-executed, and thoroughly evaluated program will have trained leaders and given teenagers some leadership experiences they would never have had otherwise. Your example of planning and administering a youth discipleship program could serve to breathe new life into other church program organizations. It could become a model of responsible service to God and His ministry. And best of all, you will know what it is to have dreamed of what God could do, and you may never hesitate to dream again.

20
Using Interns
in a Youth Discipleship
Program
Lamar Slay

Biblical Basis

"The things which you have heard from me in the presence of many witnesses, these entrust to faithful men, who will be able to teach others also" (2 Tim. 2:2, NASB). In this very familiar passage of Scripture, Paul issued a command to young Timothy that should be heeded by every youth minister. We are instructed not only to disciple others but also to teach them to do the same. One of the most effective ways to disciple youth is through the use of interns.

Our main example of interns in the New Testament is Christ Himself. As He chose the twelve men who were to be called out to be "with Him," He placed the future of the gospel, and thus the church, in their hands. In reality, they did little to further the kingdom of God while Christ was on earth, and many times they hindered His work. However, after He went back to be with the Father, they came through with high grades.

The teaching and hands-on experience that the apostles received from Christ, coupled with the power of the Holy Spirit, caused them to be the leaders in the New Testament church. Christ saw the gospel being spread to the world through His "interns."

Christ commanded us to "Go therefore and make disciples of all nations" (Matt. 28:19). If a ministry is aggressively reaching lost students for Christ, it is impossible for one or two full-time staff people to adequately follow up and disciple the new converts. Others must be enlisted to help in the process.

One source of manpower is the volunteer adults throughout our ministry. If we have effectively equipped our youth workers, they will already be involved in the discipling process. The quality of our ministry will be directly related to the quality of training we do with our volunteers. If properly trained, they are a tremendous source of help in discipling the students in your ministry. It is vitally important that they are living what they are attempting to impart to their students. If a disciple is not consistently having a daily quiet time, he or she will not be effective in teaching new disciples to spend time with God on a daily basis. Mature consistent examples are essential in the discipling process.

The second source of manpower is interns. The remainder of this chapter will deal with the philosophy of and carrying out of an intern program in the local church. While volumes could be written on this subject, the very basics will be dealt with here.

The philosophy of your intern program must be clearly defined before entering into it. An intern is not a way for a church to get inexpensive staff members. The church must realize that for the beginning period of time, every intern will be a liability. Only after a period of training, learning the people, and personal ministry will the intern become an asset. At this point, the church will begin to realize the benefits of an intern program.

The intern or interns will be the ones to receive the greatest benefit from the program. It's purpose is to train young ministers in the work of the ministry. Through this program, they can receive training that they will never get in a formal classroom setting. Just as doctors are required to go through an intern program, young ministers can be offered much the same program if churches will commit themselves to training interns. The church must see this program as a ministry that it is having in the lives of these young ministers.

Length of Internships

The length of the internships can be based on the needs and capabilities of the church. For the most part, the length of the internships can be divided into short term and long term.

The short-term internships is the most common today. It is usually based on a three-month term in the summer. Since this is the most active time of most youth ministries, it is also the best learning time for interns. While the longer-term internship may have more formal teaching times, in the shorter summer program the interns learn by doing. The goals and objectives, discussed later in this chapter, are actually demonstrated on a daily basis for the intern.

Since most people who apply for the summer internships are college students, have them arrive on the church field the week before your summer program begins. This allows you to spend a week with them in training before the busy summer begins.

While the summer program gives a church much flexibility in all areas, the program and the interns are more successful if the interns have finished at least one year of college. This helps to separate them from your high school students. The year of college has also helped to prepare them to live independently, make decisions, and to be disciplined in their personal lives.

The long-term program can range from one year to two years, but the two-year program has the most potential for the intern as well as the church. The first year is really spent in learning the church, establishing relationships, and gaining the trust of the youth. The second year can be a very productive year of ministry for the intern. By the second year, the intern is familiar with not only the students but also the adults. This enables him to work with youth as well as the adult leaders.

Due to the amount of time the youth minister will devote to a two-year internship, it is best for the intern to have finished his undergraduate degree. Attending seminary on a full- or part-time basis is a viable option. The reason for limiting the program to only two years is that by that time most interns are ready to move on to other challenges, and rightly so. Remember, our job is to train faithful youth ministers who will do likewise, not to just build a large staff.

A good administrative policy is to have an evaluation after the first three months of the two-year program. At this time, the supervisor or the intern can end the relationship if it has not worked out. No matter how you try to screen your applicants, problems may arise after the selection has been made. This preset time of evaluation and decision can be very helpful to everyone involved. The intern and the church must understand that the full commitment will be honored by both parties once the three-month evaluation has been successfully completed. Oftentimes, an intern will serve one year of his commitment and, just as he is about to become very productive, a church will call him as its youth minister. This needs to be dealt with up front, and the intern needs to be committed to the full two-year term.

Goals for the Intern

Six basic goals should be accomplished by the intern during either the three-month or two-year tenure. The degree to which these goals are accomplished will obviously be affected by the intern's length of service, the church, and her supervisors. These six areas are areas that we all seek to master as long as we are involved in ministry. The training she receives during her internship will go a long way in her development in these areas.

The first goal is for the intern to become a spiritual leader. This happens as she learns to submit to authorities and to follow directions. The intern will learn the biblical principles of developing leadership as she studies the Bible and has them modeled by her supervisor. It is important not only for her to become a spiritual leader but also to be involved in training other adults. Since this is one of the most important aspects of youth ministry, it should be given priority in the training.

The next goal is for the intern to develop Christian character and discipline. As the supervisor sees areas in the intern's life that are lacking, he should assign her special studies to strengthen those areas of her life. The intern should be taught to be disciplined in her daily time with God, Bible study, and prayer life. She also should be taught discipline in personal hygiene and physical fitness.

The third goal is for the intern to develop skills in personal evangelism and discipleship. Few interns will come to your church as aggressive soul-winners and disciplemakers. For the most part, they are not taught this in college or their churches. A basic rule is to assume nothing! The supervisor should, by example, as well as by formal teaching, help the intern develop a personal strategy for sharing her faith. She should be given weekly assignments with appointed accountability sessions.

Discipleship and follow-up techniques are essential for an effective youth ministry. The intern should not only be taught the "how to's" but also should be observed in actually discipling youth and then critiqued.

The fourth goal is to help the intern develop good interpersonal relationship skills. In the ministry, much depends on our ability to get along with others. The intern should be taught basic effective communication skills as well as counseling techniques with youth.

The fifth goal, developing effective administration skills, if effectively learned, can save the intern many hours of frustration in her future ministry. The art of delegation and personal executive skills, as well as time management and working with others in an office situation, should be studied. The intern must be held accountable for assignments made to her.

The last goal for the intern lies in the area of learning to work positively in the local church. This involves learning to work with the church staff under the leadership of the pastor as well as working with laypersons.

Training

The first week the intern is on the field should be spent in training. The training should begin with the intern's personal spiritual life. He should be taught the principle of the Spirit-filled life, how to have a daily quiet time, how to share his faith, and about spiritual warfare. These basic principles are not taught in many churches.

If multiple interns are brought on at the same time, a retreat is a good experience to help them get to know each other quickly. This initial training will lay the foundation for the ongoing weekly training. While formal classroom training is valuable, the greatest learning is going to take place as the interns observe their supervisor and fellow participants in ministry.

The intern should be challenged and taught to discipline himself to spend time in personal study, planning, and evangelism. These are areas that, if not planned for, can easily slip by unnoticed. The intern will begin to establish patterns and habits while he is with you, even if only for three months, that will stick with him for life. If, as a supervisor, you can require him to block out significant time for these three areas over a period of time, they can become very positive habits in his life.

Finances

Most churches assume that they cannot afford to have interns because of the expense involved. This is not true for many churches. The law of supply and demand comes into play in the area of internships. Very few opportunities exist for young men and women to get on-the-job training in local churches in the area of youth ministry. Many youth ministers make the mistake of accepting a call to a church without any training in how to be effective, only to find out quickly that they are unprepared for what the church wants them to do. An effective intern program can help cut the dropout rate of youth ministers.

Finances for an internship program can be handled in numerous ways. We will deal first with the short-term or summer program. The college student must view a summer internship as a part of his formal education. It is like going to summer school. In most true intern programs, the basic expenses of the intern are met, and there is no salary. As you can see, this greatly differs from a situation where a church hires an experienced person to serve as the youth minister's assistant for the summer. This can be set up on a fixed amount or on a reimbursement system. The fixed amount works best as it eliminates much unnecessary bookkeeping.

The internship program administered by me at Castle Hills First Baptist Church in San Antonio, Texas, will serve as an example, since I know it best. We paid our interns fifty dollars per week for the twelve-week term. At the end of the term, we took a churchwide love offering that was equally divided among the interns. The set amount grew steadily each year per intern, even though the number of interns also grew each year. The offering amount was a direct result of the number of families they touched during their time with us.

The majority of our interns came from within our own church. This allowed them to live and eat at home. The interns who were accepted from outside our church had to be provided with a place to live and meals. Families within our church welcomed interns into their homes. If an intern is placed in an apartment, he will need money for meals, and that can be rather expensive.

While the pay for a summer intern is low, no price can be put on the experience the intern receives. The intern program grew each year at Castle Hills, but we still had to turn down good, qualified men and women each year. In 1987, we had more than thirty applications for eight positions. This happened without any kind of brochure or advertising other than word of mouth. Many churches who currently are not involved in meeting the need for equipping youth ministers can be.

The longer, two-year internship requires more financing than the shorter program. Some churches can finance the program in their regular budget. If possible, this is good, but there are other ways.

First, a salary sufficient for a person to live on for a short period of time (two years) should be set. If a person is married, the amount needs to be adequate to care for a family. Most of our two-year interns are college graduates and attend graduate school or the seminary extension. Remember, if they had the experience you are offering them, they would be able to get a job that pays more. Their income-making ability will be greatly increased after they have served with you.

For our two-year program, we have used a system somewhat like Campus Crusade for Christ. The intern is involved in raising part of his support from friends, family, and business people before he arrives on the field. The church pays a salary and provides him with ins· rance and a yearly book allowance so he can begin to build his library. Interns explain to potential donors that they are in a training program. The commitment is for a definite period of time (two years), and the average monthly commitment is about twenty-five dollar per contributor. The money is mailed directly to the church where donor giving records are kept and mailed annually. The intern sends out a newsletter monthly to keep his supporters updated on his ministry and personal life. Personal thank-yous should also be sent for every contribution.

One area is often overlooked as far as finances are concerned. That is the area of hidden expenses in youth ministry. Since interns' pay is little, all expenses for interns must be covered for all youth activities. This may range from a few dollars for an ice-cream social to several hundred if multiple interns attend camp with the youth. One way to deal with this is by adding in to the cost per youth enough to cover your interns. The other option would be to budget enough money to cover their expenses.

Responsibilities

When planning responsibilities for interns, remember that one of our greatest failures is that we underchallenge people. Interns' duties and responsibilities should be laid out in such a way as to free the supervisor to carry out his duties. Advanced planning can eliminate the frustrating and unproductive daily, even hourly, need for the supervisor to think up ways to keep the interns busy. One idea is to assign interns on-going projects that can be evaluated and dealt with at weekly staff meetings.

At Castle Hills, each summer we assigned two interns to each Sunday School Department, one boy and one girl. Their top priority for the summer was to have a personal interview with every student on the roll in that department. Their goal was to find out if that student was a Christian, and, if not, to share Christ with him or her and give the student an opportunity to accept Christ. In order to help the interns accomplish their twelve-week goals, weekly goals were set and interns held accountable.

We divided the number of students by the number of weeks the interns were with us, less the weeks we would be out of town for camp, mission trip, and so forth, and that would be the number of students they needed to see each week. If we had not done this, the last two weeks the interns were with us they would have had fifty to sixty visits to make.

These visits were evangelistic in nature until the student gave evidence of being a Christian. The second priority of the summer interns was in the area of discipleship. From each of their departments, they were to enlist seven to ten students to meet with weekly for discipleship and evangelism training. Three to four weeks were necessary for the interns to get to know the students and enlist them. The groups met for five to six weeks and studied a topic or book chosen by the youth minister. When possible, outreach was tied into the discipleship time. It worked well to have the meeting, to go out visiting, and then all the groups meet somewhere for snacks and a sharing time about their visits.

Interns can also be of great assistance in the Youth Sunday School departments. Do not make the mistake of building your Bible teaching structure on interns, as they will leave at the end of their term. But they can be used to substitute, make announcements, and help with departmental outings. They are also great recruiters for camp and other outings.

However, interns' greatest asset to youth ministry is the time they have to spend with students, and that is where their priority should be. See your ministry through their eyes. The number of minister-hours spent in touching youth can be greatly increased through interns. Just as youth pick up your personal strengths and weaknesses, they will find themselves doing the same with the interns.

Conclusion

We as a church have a great responsibility to equip potential ministers for the gospel ministry. While the principles dealt with here are sound for any ministry, the youth ministry, in particular, can greatly benefit from an intern program. Start slowly and allow your program to grow as needed. Many youth can be reached now, and many more in the future, as your ministry is reproduced in the lives of your interns.

Resources

Dated DiscipleLife Materials

DiscipleLife Celebration

*Youth Alive** - A discipleship magazine for younger youth, grades 7-9 or ages 12-14.

*Youth Alive Leaders' Packet** - Provides help for adult and youth study leaders who use *Youth Alive.*

*Baptist Youth** - A discipleship magazine for all youth and youth leaders, grades 7-12 or ages 12-17.

*Baptist Youth Kit for Leaders** - Contains teaching/learning aids to be used with units in *Baptist Youth.*

*The Youth Disciple** - A discipleship magazine for older youth grades 10-12 or ages 15-17.

*The Youth Disciple Leaders' Packet** - Provides help for adult and youth study leaders who use *The Youth Disciple.*

*equipping youth** - Contains coordination suggestions for DiscipleLife Celebrations, relating music and worship to session material in *The Youth Disciple, Baptist Youth,* and *Youth Alive.* Other articles guide adult leaders in youth discipleship development.

Undated DiscipleLife Materials

DiscipleLife Centers

Christian Doctrine

*Direct Access: The Doctrine of the Priesthood of Believers,*** Dan Yeary
*My Salvation: Secure and Sure!*** Lavonn D. Brown
*"Our Father . . ." The Doctrine of Prayer,*** Carolyn Weatherford
*Hearers and Doers: The Doctrine of the Laity,*** Morton Rose
*Truths that Make a Difference,*** Lavonn D. Brown

Stewardship

*Choose the Best!*** Lee Davis

Christian History

*Our Heritage of Faith,*** Daniel Holcomb

Discipleship/Evangelism

*The New Connection: A Resource for Street Evangelism,*** Terry McIlvain
*The Roman Road, A Witness Training Tool,** Dean Finley, comp.
*Have a Good Life!** An evangelistic tract using Roman Road Verses
*Commitment Counseling Manual**
*Costly Commitment,*** Daniel Holcomb
*Dare to Share,*** Roy Fish
*Deepening Discipleship,*** W. L. Hendricks
*DiscipleHelps: A Daily Quiet Time Guide and Journal,** R. Clyde Hall, Jr.
*Keep Giving Away the Faith,*** Dave Bennett
*Meaningful Moments with God,*** George E. Worrell
*Youth Learning to Witness,** Joe L. Ford
*DiscipleYouth I: The Beginning,** John Hendrix
*DiscipleYouth I Leader's Guide,** R. Clyde Hall, Jr. and Joe L. Ford, Comps.
*DiscipleYouth I Kit,** R. Clyde Hall, Jr. and Joe L. Ford, Comps.
*DiscipleYouth I Notebook,** R. Clyde Hall, Jr. and Joe L. Ford, Comps.
*DiscipleYouth II Kit,** R. Clyde Hall, Jr. and Joe L. Ford, comps.
*DiscipleYouth II Retreat Booklet,** John Hendrix

DiscipleYouth II Notebook,* R. Clyde Hall, Jr. and Joe L. Ford, comps.
DiscipleYouth Songs,*** Mark Blankenship, comp.
DiscipleYouth Bible****
DiscipleYouth Prayer Pendant***
DiscipleYouth "Life" Pin***
DiscipleYouth "Life" Patch***

New Church Member Training Materials

Learning and Serving: Workbook for Youth*
Learning and Serving: Small Group Leader's Guide*

New Christian Materials

Survival Kit for New Christians, Youth Edition,** Ralph W. Neighbour, Jr.
Survival Kit - Leader's Guide for Adults, Youth, and Children**
The Journey Continues: Survival Kit 2, Youth Edition,** Ralph W. Neighbour, Jr.
A Guide for the Journey: Survival Kit 3, Youth Edition,** Thomas D. Lea

Family Life

Before You Marry,** Dan Bagby
My Home Today/Tomorrow,** Bill Bruster
Parent-Teen Relationships,* Clyde Lee Herring

Ethical Issues

Determining My Values,** Clyde Lee Herring
Cop Out, Conform, or Commit?** Ron Sisk
The Great Adventure, Building Christian Relationships,** Clyde Lee Herring

Personal Ministry

Missions Alive,** Charles Warren
God's Will, A Dynamic Discovery,** T.B. Maston
All Times Are God's Seasons,** Lela and John Hendrix

Leadership

Youth Week Idea Pak,* Jonathan Pedersen, comp./contrib.

*Youth Bible Drill/Speakers' Tournament Pak**
Your Family: Learning, Loving, Living, an equipping center module
*Youth Leadership Training Pak,*** R. Clyde Hall, Jr., comp.
A Patchwork Family, Mark and Mary Frances Henry
We Have These Treasures: A Profile of Youth Leadership Gifts
Extended Family: Combining Ages in Church Experience, Lela Hendix
Youth Becoming Leaders, Art Criscoe
*DiscipleNow Manual,** R. Clyde Hall, Jr. and Wesley Black, comps.
*Mission Trip Training Manual,** R. Clyde Hall, Jr. and Valerie Hardy,
     comps.

* Church Literature;** Convention Press;*** Broadman;**** Holman To place an order for any resource, call or write: Customer Service Center, 127 9th Ave., N, Nashville, TN 37234, 615-251-2633

Contributors

R. Clyde Hall, Jr., compiler, is manager, Youth Section, Church Training Department, The Sunday School Board of the Southern Baptist Convention, Nashville, Tennessee. He has led in the development of youth discipleship materials and programs for use in Southern Baptist churches since 1976. He is co-compiler of *Disciple Youth I* and *Disciple Youth II Kits, DiscipleHelps: A Daily Quiet Time Guide and Journal,* and *DiscipleNow Manual.* He has directed discipleship conferences for more than 100,000 youth and youth leaders. He and his wife, Mildred, have three sons: Richard, Kevin, and Edward; and one daughter, Darralyn.

Daniel Aleshire is professor of psychology and Christian education at The Southern Baptist Theological Seminary in Louisville, Kentucky. Before joining the faculty at the seminary, he worked in youth-related research at the Search Institute, and before that he had served as pastor, campus minister, and youth minister.

Billy Becham is president of Student Discipleship Ministries Fort Worth, Texas. He served for ten years as a vice-president and director of Youth Discipleship Ministries, for the International Evangelism Association. He has authored several books; among them are: *Basic Christian Discipleship, Life Style Evangelism,* and *Advanced Christian Discipleship.* He and his wife, Tracye, have one son, Billy III.

Wesley Black is assistant professor of Youth education at Southwestern Baptist Theological Seminary, Fort Worth, Texas. He has written a doctoral dissertation, a book, and other materials for discipleship courses in the field of youth discipleship. He and his wife, Sandi, are the parents of two teenagers and are active in the youth ministry of their church.

Curt Bradford is youth specialist in the Youth Section, Church Training Department of The Sunday School Board of the Southern Baptist Convention. He holds a BA in religion from Gardner Webb College and a Master of Religious Education from Southeastern Baptist Theological Seminary. He and his wife, Joyce, also are the parents of two youth, Jason and Heather, ages sixteen and twelve.

Bill Cox is the associate in the Evangelism Department of the South Carolina Baptist Convention. He has served as a minister of youth and director of "Bill Cox Abundant

Life Ministries, Inc." Cox's writings include *The Abundant Life Notebook* and accompanying *Leadership Manual.*

Art Criscoe is manager, Management Support Section, Church Training Department, The Sunday School Board of the Southern Baptist Convetion. He has written numerous articles, teaching procedures for text, coauthored *Decision Time,* and authored *Youth Becoming Leaders.*

Karen Dockrey writes full-time for youth and their leaders. She has served as minister to youth, associational youth minister, Youth Church Training coordinator, and Bible study teacher. Dockrey's books published by Broadman Press, include *Dating: Making Your Own Choices* and *Getting to Know God.* She earned her Master of Divinity from Southern Baptist Theological Seminary, Louisville, Kentucky.

Dean Finley is the national evangelism consulltant with Youth for the Home Mission Board of the Southern Baptist Convention since 1982. He has helped train over ten thousand youth leaders in the methods and processes of blending discipleship and evangelism into their ministeries. He and his wife, Beverly, have two daughters, Dawn and DeAnn.

Chuck Gartman has been in Youth ministry twenty years and has served as minister of youth, First Baptist Church Conroe, Texas, since 1977. He is a graduate of Howard Payne College, Brownwood, Texas, and Southwestern Baptist Theological Seminary, Fort Worth, Texas. He and his wife, Connie, have three daughters, Brandon, Brittany, and Brooklyn.

Martha Jo Glazner is coordinating editor, Youth Section, Church Training Department, The Sunday School Board of the Southern Baptist Convention, Nashville, Tennessee. A former youth minister, she has a Masters Degree in Christian education from Southern Baptist Theological Seminary, Master of Arts in psychology from Middle Tennessee State University, and a Bachelor of Arts from Judson College, Marion, Alabama.

John Hendrix is the Basil Manly, Jr., professor of Christian education, The Southern Baptist Theological Seminary, Louisville Kentucky. He is a proflic writer of youth discipleship materials. He and his wife, Lela, have coauthored several works. John is the author of *We Have These Treasures: A Profile of Youth Leadership Gifts.* He is a graduate of Midwestern and New Orleans Baptist Thelogical Seminaries.

Lela Hendrix is minister of students, Walnut Street Baptist Church, Louisville, Kentucky. She and her husband, John, have coauthored *All Times Are God's Seasons.* Lela has written youth discipleship materials and been actively involved in Youth ministry for more than ten years. She and John have two children, Melissa and Jud.

Jimmy Hester is design editor in the Family Ministry Department of the Sunday School Board of the Southern Baptist Convention and editor of *Living with Teenagers.* As a former minister of education and youth, and through his contact with parents and youth across the country, Jimmy has a sensitivity and knowledge of issues facing both youth and their parents.

Sam House is design editor in the Youth Section of the Church Training Department at The Sunday School Board of the Southern Baptist Convention. He has led youth ministries in Louisianna, Arkansas, and Tennessee. He and his wife, Polly, are the parents of one son, Tyler.

Wayne Jenkins is Youth specialist in the Youth Section, Church Training Department, The Sunday School Board of the Southern Baptist Convention. Jenkin's responsibilities include training adults throughout the Southern Baptist Convention to disciple youth in their local churches. He also coordinates eight national youth/youth leader discipleship conferences each year. At his church, Wayne is discipleship leader with seniors in high school.

Randy Lanford is an editor in the Youth Section, Church Training Department, The Sunday School Board of the Southern Baptist Convention and has served for more than fourteen years as a youth minister in local churches in Georgia and Texas. He is a graduate of Southwestern Baptist Theological Seminary, Fort Worth, Texas. He and his wife, Susan, have a son, Jay, and a daughter, Bethany.

Lamar Slay is the minister of students at Castle Hills First Baptist Church in San Antonio, Texas. He has been heavily involved in the development of the Texas Baptist Super Summer program and travels the country doing leadership conferences and peer pressure conferences.

W. Edward Thiele is associate professor of discipleship at New Orleans Baptist Theological Seminary in New Orleans, Louisiana. He has served as pastor of churches in Texas and Mississippi for twenty-eight years. He and his wife, Catherine, have four children.